Kumbh Mela
and
The Sadhus
The Quest for Immortality

My friend Rama Nand Tiwari, invited me to attend the Kumbh Mela at Allahabad, India in January 2007. At the same time I had the privilege of reading the manuscript for the book "Kumbh Mela and The Sadhus: The Quest for Immortality" by Badri Narain and Kedar Narain. It opened up a whole new world to me.

I have been coming to India for about ten years, and aside from seeing Sadhus in the streets, I knew nothing about their ways of living, particularly their involvement in a spiritual life and the Kumbh Mela. Indeed it was a trip of a lifetime.

The text of this book will be bringing changes to my inner life. I want to go back again to visit the holy-men and learn more about their involvement with the immortality of the soul.

Joanne W. Stephenson

Oakmont, Pennsylvania, U.S.A

21st January, 2007

Kumbh Mela
and
The Sadhus
The Quest for Immortality

Badri Narain and Kedar Narain

PILGRIMS PUBLISHING
◆ Varanasi ◆

Kumbh Mela and The Sadhus
The Quest for Immortality
by
Badri Narain and Kedar Narain

Edited ,Researched & Revised by Dr. Ashok Kumar Sharma,
Christopher N. Burchett, Eliza Miller, Atul Shukla, and
Ramanand Tiwari

Published by:
PILGRIMS PUBLISHING
Distributors in India
B 27/98 A-8, Nawabganj Road
Durga Kund, Varanasi-221010, India
Tel: 91-542- 2314060
Fax: 2312456
E-mail: pilgrims@satyam.net.in
Website:
www.pilgrimsbooks.com
www.pilgrimsonlineshop.com

Layout by Ratan Kumar, Asha Mishra & Roohi Burchett
Photographs by Badri Narain, Kedar Narain
Olaf Rocksien , Aaron McFarlin, Rama Nand Tiwari,
Akshay Kaushik, Media Centre
Paintings by B.D. Pandey, Raja Ravi Varma

ISBN: 978-81-7769-805-3

Printed in India at Pilgrims Press Pvt. Ltd. Lalpur Varanasi

Dedicated to Humanity and Nature

Contents

Foreword

Preface

Chapter 1

Introduction to Kumbh   1

Chapter 2

The Kumbh   9

The Stories of Kumbh   14

Akshayawata   32

Years of Past and Forthcoming Kumbh   41

Major Events at Past Kumbhs   42

Chapter 3

Holy Men at Kumbh Prayag   47

Chapter 4

Bathing Days at Kumbh   71

Order of Shahi for the   87

Das Naam Akharas

Chapter 5

Post Kumbh Rituals in Varanasi   89

The Tradition of Samadhi   92

Akharas at Kumbh   97

Churning of the Ocean   98

Kumbh and World Peace   101

Chapter 6

Glorious Glimpses of Haridwar and the Kumbh Mela 2010 102

Chapter 7

Kumbh, Sadhus and Salvation   134

Foreword

Kumbh is the oldest religious gathering known to man. Even looking into the deepest depths of ancient history it is almost impossible to pin a date on the exact origin. Not only was this gathering attended by holy men of all castes and creeds but by kings, nobles and the public at large, who made it a focus of pilgrimage.

Another fact that we have to realize is that this gathering was essentially one of religious personages who came together to discuss points of theology and philosophy with each other. It may be said that it was treated as a parliament or forum of religion where differences of belief and practice could be rationalized. There are many references to this gathering not only in historical records but also in the Hindu Mythology the most consistent being the references to the churning of the ocean in search of the nectar hidden within. The subsequent chase and conflict between the Gods and Demons for possession of the nectar and the four places where the pot or Kumbh containing the nectar of immortality was spilt indicate the locations of the Kumbh gatherings.

Historical references supported by already established diaries of travellers and other known figures help us to trace the origins of Kumbh. In more recent times, we of course have more detailed records of the number of people who have attended the various Kumbhs as well as the costs and preparations involved. The importance of Kumbh to the Hindu world is patently obvious when we see the numbers of the people who visit the Mela ground during the months of festivities and take part in the various auspicious occasions that occur during this period. It is also a fact that other than the occasion of Kumbh, the annual Magh fair is also held on the same ground at Prayag, and the auspicious bathing days are observed on an annual basis.

The Kumbh has now become a focal point for people the world over, many of whom visit the various Kumbhs on a regular basis. It is also surprising that there are those from the west who have adopted the Hindu way of life and who camp at this fair, bringing with them their own followers who have gathered around them. Though this gathering was related to the holy men and some also say the Gods as well as the kings and queens of ancient history, it has now become an international event closely watched by the world at large.

Christopher N Burchett

Preface

Kumbh in Sanskrit refers to a 'pot' or a pitcher and the word *mela* in Sanskrit means a 'gathering' or a 'fair'. The historic origin of the *Kumbh Mela* dates back to Vedic times when the gods and demons were fighting for a pot of nectar (*Amrit Kumbh* — the nectar of immortality). Lord Vishnu, disguising himself as an enchantress, Mohini, seized the nectar from the demons. While fleeing from them, Lord Vishnu passed the nectar on to his winged mount, Garuda. The demons finally caught up with Garuda and in the ensuing struggle, a few drops of the precious nectar fell at Allahabad, Nasik, Haridwar and Ujjain. Since then, the *Kumbh Mela* has been held in all these places, alternatively, every 12 years.

It is believed that to participate in the *Kumbh* is to gain Salvation, getting rid of ones burden of accumulated sins. For thousands of years, people from all castes, religious beliefs, and social levels have gathered at the *Kumbh Mela*. According to the *Vishnu Puran,* the *Bhagvad Puran,* the *Mahabharata* and the *Ramayan*, the *Kumbh Parva* is being celebrated since pre-historic times. There is no such extravaganza like the *Kumbh Mela* anywhere else in the world.

The *Kumbh Mela* begins on the full moon night (*Purnima*) of the month of Paush, occurring roughly between 22 December and 20 January. While the *Kumbh Mela* is held at Haridwar, Ujjain and Nasik every four years, the Kumbh at Prayag has a special significance. The *Kumbh Mela* is marked by the fact that it is held at the banks of holy rivers every 12 years. In Prayag, however, it is held on the banks of the rivers Ganges-Yamuna, with the underground Saraswati joining in. In Haridwar it is held at Ganges, in Ujjain at river Kshipra and in Nasik at the Godavari. A great fair is held on these occasions on the banks of these rivers with a huge congregation of devoted pilgrims. The Prayag Kumbh is also considered to be the most significant because it marks the direction of wisdom or light. This is the place where the sun, symbolizing wisdom, rises.

It is noteworthy that in the year 2001 at Prayag, approximately 60 million pilgrims came to the *Mahakumbh*, a world record for a human gathering. Then in 2010 in Haridwar, the numbers reached up to eighty million and yet again established a new record.

For the first time in the history of *Sanatana Dharma,* the idol of Lord *Tirupati Balaji* was brought from South India to Haridwar for bathing in the Ganges. Also, the divine light (*Jyoti*) of *Tripur Sundari*, the *Shakti* of Lord Shiva was brought from district Kamroop of Assam to the

Haridwar *Kumbh*. If seen from the perspective of *Tantra Vidya* (Occult Science), this is a very blissful coincidence. On this grand occasion, personalities like His Holiness the Dalai Lama, Yoga Guru Baba Ramdev, Swami Chidanand Saraswati of Parmarth Niketan, former Deputy Prime Minister L. K. Advani, Uttarakhand Chief Minister Dr. Ramesh Pokhariyal 'Nishank' and other prominent personalities from different fields gathered at Rishikesh and resolved to conserve and protect Mother Ganga.

For the Haridwar *Kumbh Mela* 2010 all the responsibilities were taken over by the Chief Minister Dr. Ramesh Pokhariyal, who oversaw the event in an excellent and effective manner. His associates Sri Madan Kaushik (Minister for Urban Development, Tourism, Sugarcane Development, Sugar Industry and Excise) and Sri Subash Kumar (Principal Secretary to the CM) approved a budget of Rs. 5.65 billion for the *Kumbh Mela* from which 321 building projects were completed. 3500 security personnel from Uttar Pradesh, 10,000 from Uttarakhand, and 5,500 from other states were deployed. With the use of 87,000 vehicles (heavy and light) and 200 trains, the pilgrims, tourist and others arrived and departed. For the first time in the history of the *Kumbh Mela,* lifeguards saved around 800 lives from drowning. People from 140 countries gathered at the Haridwar *Kumbh*, including approximately 2,200 media persons working in 30 national and international languages. By providing the food, camps and transportation facilities to eighty million people, the State of Uttarakhand has set an example of cooperation, coordination, harmony, and patience.

After participating in Haridwar *Kumbh Mela*, citizens of all countries would have surely learned and experienced some new things, which will hopefully affect the peace, prosperity and stability of every nation of the world. We believe that the *Kumbh Mela* will work as a 'life-giving herb' (*Sanjeevini*) for the future of Humanity which is deep in the clutches of war, exploitation, poverty, hunger, racism, ill-health, etc. The *Kumbh Mela* should be bestowed with the Noble Peace Prize.

Editorial Board

Chapter 1
Introduction

The Kumbh as a *Tirtha* (holy place of pilgrimage) is a sacred occasion of collective consciousness where all have the same thought and intention to observe God in the moment. The Kumbh holds the presence of all the Tirthas. It is an identified infinite power for the use of the masses. Kumbh combines an assembly of royalty, householders, ascetics and renunciates on one religious platform, irrespective of background, caste or creed. It is holy to all. It is Prayag.

No religious congregation in the world's history has achieved such numbers as the Kumbh in India. No mass pilgrimage to any other *Tirtha* is enriched with the capacity to provide such qualities in full measure—salvation, peace, satisfaction and much more—as Kumbh at Prayag on the bank of the holiest of the holy rivers, the Ganga. The feeling gained by the devotee here is beyond that gained at any other city or at the temple of any other God. The satisfaction gained by devotees after a holy dip during Kumbh is much greater than any bath anywhere else on any sacred day. Kumbh is above any individual sect nor is there any devotee who is not allowed to participate.

Only during colonial times there was restriction imposed. The devotees in India who took a holy bath at the confluence of Prayag during Kumbh in order to satisfy their religious faith, were at that time, had to pay the severe taxes levied by the British Colonial Rulers. Every man, even the poorest beggar, was asked to pay a tax of one rupee for the liberty to take a bath there.

Kumbh is something to be celebrated, enjoyed and experienced by all. Goswami Tulsidasa has written in praise of the religious spot of Prayag where the Kumbh is held and he expressed his inability to explain the grace and impact of the holy city Prayag, in his verse in *Ram Charit Manasa*; 'Ko Kahi Sake Prayag Prabhau' asks 'who can completely explain the grace of Prayag?'

Kumbh Prayag, 1991

Kumbh is widely termed as a *Parva,* a holy event, and sometimes the greatest of all sacred events, a *Maha Parva.* Kumbh is an auspicious moment, a fraction of time when the Planets in the sky are in a leveraged position to influence the inner soul of living creatures.

Kumbh Parva first appears in the Vedic religious texts, where it is written *Mrityor Ma Amritam Gamaya,* meaning let nature move humanity from death to immortality. *Amrita* (nectar) implies beyond any death.

Kumbh commemorates that *Amrita*—Elixir of Immortality. The quest for Amrita Kumbh is associated with the story of the churning of the ocean and subsequent fight between Gods and Demons chasing each other around heaven and earth after the pitcher containing Amrita. The pitcher containing the elixir of immortality was the vessel called Kumbh. We find another mention of Amrita in the holy text of the Ramayana, where the demon king Ravana held Nectar within his Navel.

Kumbh Prayag

An astronomical combination of the planets causes the holy event, *Kumbh Parva*. The Gods secured the pot *(Kumbh/Kalasha)* and protected it from breaking or being taken over by Demons. However, during the subsequent chase, few drops of the nectar spilled out.

These zones where the nectar spilled out of the Kumbh became the earthly centres where the auspicious moment Kumbh Parva is to be memorially observed. Two of the zones are on the bank of the river Ganga and the Kumbh at Prayag is ranked as the most important spiritual and religious gathering anywhere. The monks call it *Rajrajeshwari*.

There are five *Parva* days for sacred bathing during Kumbh Prayag within a period of 30 days in the month of *Magh* as per the Hindu calendar.

Yet the Naga Sanyasis celebrate Kumbh for a period of just ten days and join only three of the Parva days of mass bathing in the holy river. They maintain the tradition of Naga monks who, during the period of King Harshawardhana of Kannauj, in 700 A.D., received donations only up to ten days within a period of 75 days of the Kumbh at Prayag.

Meditation, idol worship, sacred bathing at the river confluence, offering of food to one's ancestors in heaven, *Pinda,* and giving charity are the main religious activities during Kumbh. For some it is simply a one day visit for a holy dip or a *Shahi Snana,* for others to simply admire sights of the moment and for yet others Kumbh may be a rush to make donations to both seek salvation in this existing life and secure a place in heaven after death.

Paintings by B.D. Pandey

Kumbh is related to an age old tradition of mass bathing in the river, as if it was the urn of immortality, on the banks of the sacred rivers Ganga, Sangam (confluence of Ganga, Yamuna, Sarawati), Kshipra and Godawari. It demonstrates the faith and belief of the people who move out to wash away the burden of accumulated sins, intending to cross the river of punishment and further seek an answer to the mortality.

Kumbh is to guide the humans through the conflict between the immortality of the soul against the mortal existence of the body, made of the *Panch Tatwas* (five elements, air, earth, fire, water and sky). It invites human gathering on an open stage to frame rules for social behaviour, and discuss and implement them on the society as a whole, irrespective of caste, creed, faith or religion. The Kumbh, above all, reveals the immortality of their souls to the mortal living creatures on this earth. The constituents of religion, spiritualism, the holy-tree, the holy-men, the holy-rivers and the holiest of the holy-places of pilgrimage form the platform of immortality.

In other words, Kumbh forms a place for the salvation of mankind who wish to be free of the cycle of birth and death.

Kumbh is not only the world's largest outdoor congregation of religious faith and the biggest Hindu festival, but as well the largest human gathering of any type, in terms of the number of people who participate. The Kumbh has a periodicity based on astrological calculations. It is called a *Mela* or fair for Hindu pilgrimage and since before recorded time, it occurs on every twelfth year at four sacred spots - Allahabad, Haridwar, Ujjain and Nasik.

Pt. Jawahar Lal Nehru, the first Prime Minister of free India, in his book the *Discovery of India* states, '…even at that time, those Melas were considered to be much older and it can not be said when they began…'

Chapter 2
The Kumbh

Kumbh Mela reveals the drive for unity amongst all people on this earth. The mix of spiritual leaders, religious storytellers, and monks under various religious banners, all appearing on this communal platform advocate the singleness of the god whom humanity worships with different names.

That the Akharas, some with capitalistic and others with socialistic or communistic patterns of administration and management, come together at Kumbh to discuss, debate and agree on policy, is a demonstration of the oldest form of religious tolerance and democracy on the globe. The tradition of charity at Kumbh by the rulers to the public, by the rich to the poor, in the Akharas to the ascetics emphasizes the economic theory of distribution of wealth amongst the community for higher spiritual purpose.

The symbol and astronomy of Kumbh

The symbol of Kumbh is a *Kalasha* or a gold pot containing heavenly nectar for survival of all creatures. Mythologically it relates to all water and liquid on earth. The nectar is also called *Amrita* or the elixir of immortality. The Kalasha or metal pot containing the liquid in the form of a river's sacred water is also considered a deity as God of the Water in the universe. The Juna Akhara uses a Kalasha-a pot, as their mobile deity, calling their portable altar, *Varuna Dewata*, after the water lord Varuna.

The Kalasha is an essential part of any auspicious occasion, for example a marriage ceremony or a Yagya in a Hindu family. During death rites, the pot containing the water is broken when the dead body is moved from the house for the final rites at the cremation ground . Then another earthen pot containing water is hung on a Peepal tree for ten days.

God Ganesha by Raja Ravi Varma

Haridwar Kumbh 1840 (Pilgrims collection)

The occasion of the gathering for Kumbh is based on stories from the *Rig Veda* related to the placement of the planets in astrological signs. The favourable zodiacal placement of the Kumbh planets affects the solar activity on earth and is beneficial to all creatures, especially at those spots along the sacred river banks during Kumbh. It is said that the greatest outpouring of spiritual power lands on earth at the meeting point of the Ganga, Yamuna and Saraswati rivers, the Sangam at Prayag-Allahabad *(Rajrajeshwari)*. The less mentioned, invisible third river, Saraswati, is not of this earth, either because it dried up long ago or it never actually existed in the physical dimension.

Religious texts for followers of the Sanatana Dharma narrate the stories

Kalash

of the gods and demons attempt to search for the nectar at the bottom of the sweet water sea to conquer mortality. According to these ancient scripts, astrological combinations cause the time of Kumbh to occur. Kumbh occurs when Jupiter, a teacher of the Hindu Gods in heaven, moves into one of the zodiac sign of Aries, Taurus, Leo and Scorpio. Astronomical calculations of planetary orbits show the planet Jupiter, *Brahaspati*, cycles

Kumbh Prayag 1996

into Aries (Mesh Rashi) at the same time as the Sun and the Moon are in the sign of Capricorn (Makar Rashi) about every 12 years. Ancient religious texts state that the Kumbh occurs at twelve spots within the zones of heaven, earth and the underworld, with four spots in each. Ardha Kumbh and Kumbh occur at the holy Indian cities of (1) Prayag (Allahabad) (2) Haridwar (3) Ujjain and (4) Nasik

Smudra Manthan (Painting by B.D. Pandey)

Pilgrims at Kumbh Prayag 2001 (Olaf Rocksien)

Kumbh cycle and astrological position
Kumbh Mela Place, River, Direction, Hindu/Month, Years/Dates, <u>Planets/Zodiac signs</u>

East - *Kumbh Mela at Prayag - Sangam - Allahabad* Rivers Ganga, Yamuna and Saraswati. Magha/January 1989, 2001, 2012, 2024
<u>*Jupiter in Aries/Taurus, Sun and Moon in Capricorn*</u>

Ardha Kumbh also at Sangam-Allahabad at mid-cycle after 6 years, in Magha/January when <u>*Jupiter in Scorpio , Sun and Moon in Capricorn*</u>

North - *Kumbh Haridwar* at River Ganga in Caitra/Mar-Apr 1986, 1998, 2010, 2021
<u>*Jupiter in Aquarius, Sun in Aries and Moon in Cancer*</u>

also Ardha Kumbh Haridwar, 6 years, Caitra/Mar-Apr
<u>*Jupiter in Leo, Sun in Aries*</u>

West - *Kumbh Ujjain* at River Kshipra in Vaisakha/April 1980, 1992, 2004, 2016.
<u>*Jupiter in Leo, Sun in Aries and when Jupiter and Moon are in Libra*</u>

South - *Kumbh Nasik* at River Godavari in Bhadrapada/Aug-Sep 1980, 1992, 2003, 2015.
<u>*Jupiter, Sun and Moon in Libra*</u>

Maha Kumbh
There is a complete astronomical rotation of the Kumbh planets after every one hundred and forty four years. This causes the extra significance of Maha (Great) Kumbh, at the planetary return after twelve successive Kumbh Melas. As there are twelve zodiacal signs and a day has two sets of twelve planetary hours. So does Kumbh have a period of twelve years, a Maha Kumbh planetary rotation is 144 years or 12x12 years.

Bathing at Kumbh (Olaf Rocksien)

The Stories of Kumbh

The word *Amrita* means *not dead*. It means immortal or one immune to death. The earthly occasion of the Kumbh celebrates and symbolises the shower of nectar *Amrita* which drops from heaven into the sacred river water streams on earth. The faith behind the *Kumbh Parva* in India is the transmission of immortality to the living creatures on the earth.

There are only two stories on Kumbh in the Hindu religious texts. The first and primary story, *Maharshi Durwasa* or *Samudra Manthan*, narrates the exploitation of the sweet water sea named *Chhiroda Samudra*, the search of Amrita by the gods and demon brothers wanting immunity from death. The second, lesser known story is *Kadru Vinita*. Both stories are related to the outcome of internal disputes among the successors of Maharshi Kashyapa, one of the seven great Rishis.

The story of the *Samudra Manthana* depicts that with a joint pact to equally share the findings, the most powerful Gods and Demons in the universe agreed to churn the sea water from the bottom where the sweet nectar was hidden along with wealth and power. It was under the advice of Lord Brahma, the creator, that the sea was to be churned using the

Kumbh Prayag (Olaf Rocksien)

Images of the female deities Ganga, Yamuna and Saraswati with the child forms of Brahma, Vishnu and Mahesh at Kumbh

mountain Mandara or *Mandarachal Parvata* as a churning rod.

The rope to be coiled around the churning rod was the mightiest and the longest serpent, the King of Serpents *Vasuki Naga*, who was in the bowels of the earth. Lord Vishnu incarnated himself into a tortoise which was called as *Kachchhapa Awatar*, and brought the mountain to the sea bearing the load of the mountain on his back.

The churning process resulted in foam for the first five years, wine after a period of eight years, the white cow Kamdhenu at the end of the ninth year, the white Airawata elephant at the end of the tenth year and the seven-headed white horse called Uchchaishrava in year eleven.

The revelations continued with the Apsara, dancing girls of heaven, after eleven years three months and the moon after twelve years three months. The churning also resulted in a deadly poison called the *Kala*

Churning of the ocean to avail Kumbh Kalash (Painting B.D. Pandey)

Koota Visha, at the end of thirteen years three months, which started killing the Gods and the Demons.

In answer to the gods petition, the supreme Lord Shiva collected the poison and held it to his neck. The adverse effect of the poison caused his neck to turn blue, giving the great God the name of *Neela Kantha* which means "blue necked."

The bow was revealed after churning for 14 years 3 months, the conch after 15 years 3 months, and the *Parijatak* flower tree after 16 years 3 months. Just one month later, after 16 years 4 months of churning, out came the jewel *Kaustabha Mani,* Jyestha (the goddess of poverty) and Laxmi (the goddess of wealth). Twelve years later, at the end of 30 years 5 months churning, out came Dhanwantari holding the Kumbh containing the Amrita immortality elixir. The *Kartika Mahatmya* describes the total period of 30 years 5 months, as being per the life of Lord Brahma. It is assumed that one day in the life of god Brahma equals roughly one year of our time.

The Gods and the Demons started fighting with each other upon seeing the nectar, in a frenzy to take hold of the Kumbh containing the nectar. The king of the gods Indra, directed his son Jayanta to capture the pitcher and to save it. Jayanta secured the Kumbh vessel and sought a safe place to hide it. He ran around the entire universe being followed by demons for twelve days during which he rested at  twelve spots in heaven, underworld and on this earth. The four places where he stopped on this earth are Haridwar, Nasik, Ujjain and Prayag in India along the sacred rivers Ganga, Godawari, Kshipra, and at the confluence of the rivers Ganga, Yamuna and Saraswati respectively. As Jayanta ran, few drops of Amrita spilled out from the Kumbh at those four places in the Mrityu Loka and at eight other centres in the Deva Loka and Patala Loka worlds where the Gods reside.

The period of twelve days for the Gods equals twelve years of human time, hence the Kumbh happens each successive twelve years. The zones where the urn spilled became centres where the Kumbh Parva, the auspicious moment, is to be observed. The fortunate combination of the planets as Gods secured the pitcher of Amrita *Kumbh Kalasha* from spilling, breaking or being hijacked and inspired Jayanta against fear.

The story of Kadru Vinita and how the snakes got his forked tongue
Kadru and Vinita, twin sisters, the daughters of Daksha Prajapati, were

The Gods carrying Nectar Pot (Painting B.D. Pandey)

Mohini appears out of the Ocean (painting B.D. Pandey)

married to Kashyap Rishi. Kadru became the mother of the snake family and Vinita the mother of the most powerful bird Garuda. Kadru and Vinita while out walking, caught a glimpse of the white horse jewel and made a bet about the colour of the horse's tail. Kadru bet for black, Vinita bet for the tail to be white. The loser had to become slave of the winner. Kadru asked her sons, the snakes, to cover the tail of the horse and change the appearance to black.

As a result of this mischief, Vinita lost the bet and became a slave to the snake family. To stop this slavery, Garuda, the son of Vinita, had to bring Amrita for the snakes. The Amrita was protected by the king of the Gods-Indra, who agreed to hand over Amrit Kalash to Garuda on the terms that he will not allow his snake cousins to drink the Amrita.

Garuda brought the Amrita Kalash to the snakes camp and placed it on Kusha, a sharp-edged grass. The snakes, before drinking sacred Amrita, attended themselves to a ritual bath. Meanwhile, Indra reached the snake camp and escaped with the Kalash. The hopeful snakes started licking the Kusha grass where the Amrita Kalash had been. The sharp grass caused their tongues to bifurcate. From this time Kusha is considered to be pious.

Another extension of this story narrates a fight in which Indra attacked

Garuda four times resulting in the spilling of Amrita at the four earthly spots where we celebrate Kumbh Mela.

The Kumbh fair at Allahabad
The holy days, number of the pilgrims and the Mela budget

The Kumbhs for stationary camping usually continue for four weeks. The peak religious moments are on the five auspicious days when bathing at the *Sangam* (confluence) takes place. The sacred days of bathing are (1) *Makara Sankranti*, (2) *Pausha Purnima*, (3) *Mauni Amavasya*, (4) *Basant Panchami*, and (5) *Maghi Purnima*. Some believe the sixth day for sacred bathing at Kumbh is (6) *Maha Shiva Ratri*.

The numbers of pilgrims who visit Kumbh Prayag continues to increase over the years. Amongst the bathing days, *Mauni Amavasya* has the greatest significance and therefore, attracts huge crowds of pilgrims who come for only a day or two.

The total number of pilgrims crowding on and around the bathing ghat varies on the different *Parva* days, the highest being on the Mauni Amavasya Day. The Kumbh 1906 recorded 260,000 pilgrims at Prayag whereas Kumbh 2001 recorded 10.2 million pilgrims who visited it on a single day.

Mohini entertains both Devas and Asuras (painting B.D. Pandey)

The total inflow of pilgrims during 44 days at Maha Kumbh Prayag in 2001 was recorded to have 74.4 million persons. The 1989 Kumbh Prayag recorded the attendance at *Maha Kumbh* which, after a cycle of 144 years, at 13.6 million pilgrims in a single day. About 3.6

Pilgrims at Ardha Kumbh Prayag (Olaf Rocksien)

million pilgrims lost their companions in the Mela ground. The Kumbh city Prayag recorded an entry rate of about 13,000 pilgrims per minute and those who became lost from companions counted at the rate of 20 pilgrims per minute.

The bathing rate of the pilgrims at the Sangam in 1989 was recorded as 300,000 pilgrims per hour. The bathing rate by the boats was recorded at 40,000 persons per hour. The inflow of the pilgrims toward the Sangam was recorded at an average rate of 600,000 persons per hour. The Mela budget soared from 92,094 rupees in Indian currency in 1906 to 770 million in the 1989 Kumbh. Kumbh Prayag 2001 had a budget of 200 million rupees.

Bathing at Kumbh Prayag 1996

According to Hindu mythology, 'Prayagraja', the holy city, visits Varanasi for a holy dip in the river Ganga after every Kumbh and Ardha Kumbh at Prayag. The Kumbh Mela budget informally makes a provision for this post ceremonial occasion.

Charity seeker at Ardha Kumbh Prayag 2001

Saints and Kalpawasis

There are the devotees known as *Kalpawasis* who join the Kumbh and stay as novitiates in tents in the sacred land area for a period of thirty days. Such householder pilgrims renounce their household facilities during the month they stay here. They take a sacred dip three times a day and benefit by listening to the Sermons (religious lectures) in different *Pandals*.

A part from religious rites at Sangam, the Kumbh tradition includes visiting the wide assortment of assembled saints, sages and renunciates. The holy-men deliver darshan blessings, religious discourses and debate on spiritual matters. Kumbh has always been about tolerant religious discourse and celebration.

Great holy personalities like Jagadguru Shankaracharya, Tulsidas, Lord Buddha, Guru Nanaka, Chaitanyadev, Kabir, Guru Govind Singh, Swami Dayananda and many others have attended this holy occassion in the past. The saints TuKa Rama, Ramananda and Ramanujacharya preached here and the great old teacher Kumrila Bhatta met Shankaracharya. At Kumbh, the spiritually hungry pilgrims may join the saints as they all travel on holy pilgrimage.

Maa Ganga and her son leaving King Shantanu

Painting by Raja Ravi Varma

The tradition of Mundana, Snaana and Daana at Kumbh

The most auspicious of the religious rituals for the householder pilgrims at Kumbh Prayag are *Mundana* - shaving of the head at the river bank, *Snana* - sacred bathing in the river and *Daana* - making donation or gift of charity at the Sangam.

The Mundana is performed by a pilgrim for the sake of the salvation of one's ancestors in heaven. It is an after death rite to be performed by the successors of a deceased person, especially by male family member. As for women, only widows may be tonsured (head shaved bald) on the passing of their husbands. Every hair shaved away in the river stream is supposed to lessen one's eternal punishment, bearing away the sins of the past ten thousand years.

To fulfill one's voluntary sacrifice, made as gifts of land, animals, food or money to the Brahmin priests called *Panda, Purohita or Ghatia*, one takes a holy dip in the river's confluence then recites and accepts the words of promise for a sacrifice as per the *Sankalpa Mantra*.

The tradition of giving charity to secure pleasure and a place in heaven dates back to at least the 7th century A D. when the king of Kannauj, Harsh Vardhana, emptied his coffers every six years while standing in the stream at Prayag Sangam. After distributing his entire wealth, he begged from his sister two pieces of clothing to wear. In a more recent act of royal generosity, the Maharani (queen) Dowager of Tiperrha at the 1918 Kumbh Mela, donated an elephant to her priest at the Sangam confluence.

The most common sacrificial gift made by the pilgrims is *Gau Daana* (gift of a cow). The Ghatias, religious guides and caretakers of devotee's belongings at the bathing Ghats, tie cows and calves to wooden platforms to help devotees who wish to make a symbolic donation of a cow. The cow helps the soul to cross the river of punishment called *Baitarni* after death if *Gau Daana* was made. Even saints and monks make *Dana*, donations, inside their Akharas after the great bathing procession *Shahi*. Sanyasis, particularly the Nagas, perform the *Mundana Sanskara* of the newly initiated monks at the Sangam during the Kumbh and Ardha Kumbh.

Magh Mela and the ritual of Magh Snana.
A 30 days fair and bathing ritual at Prayag
The Kumbh and Ardha Kumbh bathing rituals at Prayag both take place in the month of Magh, i.e., the eleventh month of the Hindu calendar. The Kumbh Parva and Magh Snana are both sacred bath rituals yet they differ from one another. The Kumbh Parva consists of five distinct main bathing events, whereas the Magh Mela is thirty continuous days of sacred bathing. The Kumbh happens once in twelve years, rotating among four places and the Magh Snaana is an annual event in only Prayag. For both events, a temporary city stands on the sandy bed at the river confluence and attracts the householders who dwell as home comfort renunciates in the tent homes. The tradition of *Kalpwas* is a yearly event during which the householders vow to follow the life of a novitiate for thirty days.

Mundan Sanskar

Magh Mela is based on the astronomical observations of the great Indian astrologer, Vessametta, of about 3468 BC, who set in motion the tradition of **Magh Snana.** Authors like S. B. Roy (*Early Aryans of India 3100-1400 B.C.* p. 55) are of the opinion that the great bath on the new moon day of Magh called the *Maghi Amavasya Snaana* goes back to the hoary antiquity of the pre-Harappan age in India. Another mention of Magh Mela dates back to 288 A.D. in India, when astronomy became solar. A third assumption is that it was organised by emperor Harsha when the Mela period was recorded as continuing for eighty-five days.

Bathing at Kumbh Prayag 2001

The Ganga Poojana rituals prior to Kumbh

The government administrators of the Kumbh fair at Prayag ensure a peaceful end to the coming Mela by following a ritual of worshiping the sacred river Ganga at the confluence before commencing any sort of preparations on the site. The Mela officers, religious heads, officially recognised priests and others chants hymns and offer milk and flowers etc., to the river stream from a platform at the confluence bed. The ritual is sometimes held in the month of November when the river bed recedes to its inner sanctum (*Garbha Griha*) after the flood at Prayag. The land area

Sapt Rishis Painting by Raja Ravi varma

vacated by the rivers Ganga and Yamuna will be allotted to different Akharas. The Akhara heads join the *Pooja*, then are invited to discuss their requirements of the land area.

It is believed that the success of Kumbh Mela depends on the mercy of the river Ganga. Activities related to Mela management and implication of the forecasted plans, judging the quantum of water in the river and its estimated level, estimated volume of the crowd, measurement of the sandy area, allocation of Mela budget, etc., all begin after the ritual of *Ganga Poojana.*

In order to ensure massive cooperation and coordination among the government departments in favor of the unknown future pilgrims visiting the land, the administrative intentions pertaining to management and control are reviewed on the eve of *Ganga Poojana*. A Mela officer deputed for the purpose is settled in a Mela office just above the Bandh. The Mela office gives the final shape to the temporary city called Kumbh Nagar meant to house the tens of millions coming for the religious gathering.

The activities related to Mela administration and management are numerous, extending well beyond the allotment of sandy river beds to the Priests, Pandas, Barbers, Akharas, Media and Kalpawasis. There are multiple needs for crowd management, such as recognition of entry and exit points of the Mela, a strategy for diversion and directional flow of incoming hordes at the bathing zones, while having arrangements for easy

Ganga Arti: His Holiness the Dalai Lama and others (Rama Nand Tiwari)

access of influential people and VIPs to the confluence of the river. The accommodations for hundreds of millions of pilgrims, living in a short-term city, requires planning and building of roads, installation of electricity and lighting, potable water supply and hygiene, civil amenities, supplies and transportation, as well as coordination among emergency services departments and military, control of suspect activities and crime, health facilities including containment of any

Pooja at Kumbh

contagious diseases which may occur in such a crowded environment and of course, the fixing of revenue and taxes such as standardisation of boat and rickshaw charges, etc.

The sacred rivers at Sangam and the Sangam scene

The confluence of the two sacred river streams forms a triangular curvature of religious significance for those who follow *Sanatana Dharma*. At every such junction the triangular area is known as a Sangam. Sangam at Prayag holds the greatest religious import and attracts the largest grouping of humanity coming together in any single place for any purpose, when flocks of pilgrims gather to bath.

The 2001 Kumbh recorded entry of 30 million pilgrims on a single day. This figure is equal to approximately three percent of the total population of the nation of India. 300 million was the total attendance over the most extended time period.

Holy men at Kumbh Prayag 2001

Religious Rituals on the River Bank during Kumbh

There are rituals called *Sanskara,* which are practiced by Hindus from birth to death, and are best performed in the presence of the sacred river Ganga. The religious rites performed with the holy river water are listed as:

1. The holy bath (*Snaana*),
2. Meditation (*Dhyana*),
3. Visualising an idol of the God (*Darshana*),
4. Donation of a cow (*Gau Daana*),
5. Offering made during an Eclipse (*Doma Ka Daana*),
6. Vow to offer (*Sankalpa*),
7. Worship (*Puja*),
8. Prayer (*Paatha*),
9. To walk around a temple clockwise (*Parikrama*),
10. Fasting (*Vrata*),
11. Listening to religious stories (*Katha*),
12. Chanting of holy *Mantras*,
13. Offering a sacrifice (*Daana*),
14. Newlywed's rituals (*Ganga Pujaiaya*),
15. Offering holy water to one's ancestors in heaven (*Tarpana*),
16. Water Samadhi *(Jal Samadhi)*
17. Tonsure/Shaving of the head (*Mundana*)
18. Spreading the ashes of a corpse (*Asthi*),
19. Offerings of food rituals for one's ancestors (*Pinda, Shraddha*),
20. Prayer for one's wishes (*Manokamana Siddhi*),
21. After worship gifts (*Prasada*),
22. Applying a sectarian marking to the forehead (*Tilaka*),
23. Offering of the flame of an oil lamp (*Deep Daana* and *Aarti*),
24. Washing away one's sins (*Shuddhi Snaana*),
25. Gaining the benefit of Salvation (*Mukti*),
26. Immersion of an idol (*Murti Visarjana*)

Photo by Ramanand

Kumbh Mela and the Sadhus

Approaching the Kumbh

Along the approaches to the river water's edge are shops selling food stuffs and items of devotional aid. The devotees after a sacred bath carry the gift items in their hands as a token of their sacred journey. Pilgrims who want souvenirs of the sacred river water, fill a metal or a plastic container. They go sprinkling Ganga water and throwing other items of sacrifice on the cloths spread on the ground by the charity seekers and beggars.

The visitors' entry can be seen as a wave of human heads, increasing round the clock on a Parva day or a day before. There is no advertisement or call to invite them to Kumbh. The priests simply read the Hindu

almanac called a *Patra* or a *Panchanga* declaring the time and day of the holy moment and the devotees move. Among the crowd some halt temporarily and camp under open sky with their belongings. They move towards Sangam in small groups, carrying their belongings on their heads and staying at different points.The one day pedestrian pilgrims often link with devotees halting in a religious Pandal to stay with them. The crowd at Sangam includes the one day travellers, Kalpawasis, priests, Pandits/Purohits, police, members of voluntary services, various organized groups, guides, foriegn tourists, media, Ghatiyas, boatmen, the suppliers of milk and flowers at the river bank, barbers, government servants, beggars and holy men. In individual groups they throng to the Sangam bed where it is hard for anyone to escape from the great rush pushing from behind. The pilgrims moving in the crowd somehow find their way back to join their groups who await their return after a sacred bath. Anyone sitting on the ground would be in danger of being trampled underfoot at the water's edge. VIPs do not face the crowd as they take

Shankaracharya bathing at the Sangam Kumbh Prayag 2001

advantage of bathing inside a *Bajara* (house-boat secured with a hanging platform).

Devotional songs around the clock fill the environs with a spiritual mood. In the bedlam, the devotees loudly say out the deities' names: *Yamuna Maiya Ki Jai, Ganga Maiya Ki Jai, Triveni Ki Jai, Tirtha Raja Ki Jai, Prayag Raja Ki Jai, etc.*

The heightened atmosphere of devotion formed by the enormous wave of humanity at the sacred river streams impacts the devotees emotional satisfaction beyond any group worship activity performed anywhere else on any other sacred day.

The holy river on a Kumbh Parva day carries in her waves the nectar of immortality for her devotees, breaking divisions between rich and poor,

Pandal at Kumbh

sages and house-holders and all creeds or castes, at least during the Kumbh.

The crowd dried off after their holy dip in the river would visit Patalpuri temple at some distance from the confluence, inside the fort on the banks of the river Yamuna. Here the giant stone-built idols stand witness to the glory of this sacred land in the past. Devotees take the benefit of touching the main shrines of the deities for a blessing, self-purification and to secure a place in heaven. A newly grown banyan tree is growing to a large size at the vantage point of the river confluence bed. At a very short distance is a Peepal tree. The trees at this point are worshipped by the daily bathers.

Akshayawata, the immortal tree of heaven and the Kumbh at Prayag
The holy tree in the religious texts.

According to the most revered religious texts, the immortal tree of heaven *Akshayawata* broke through earth's crust at Prayag and spread around. Unlike the God Lord Shiva in the form of a phallic *Lingam* at Varanasi, the deity God Shiv appeared here in the form of a tree. It is only here at Prayag that Lord Shiva is symbolised in the banyan tree as a pillar of light around which the entire universe revolves. Lord Vishnu rests on the leaves of the tree as an infant baby who recreates the entire universe after the final day of destruction (*Pralaya*). This particular tree at the Sangam is also believed to remain with its leaves and even float above the watery world after the final day of destruction, *Pralaya*. The immortal tree of heaven, *Akshayawata*, at Prayag Raja once covered an area of five *Yeozana* (measurement of distance), with its one hundred branches as described in the *Prayag Mahatmya Shatadhyayi* (a holy book) which glorifies the grace of the city. At that time, the trunk of the tree was not visible through the branches. The holy stream of the river Yamuna was south facing the tree.

The epics *Ramayana* and *Mahabharata* relating to the Dwapara and Treta Yugas tell of a period of about two million years, giving references to the historical and political events and the confluence of the three great rivers of India at Prayag Raja. A reference in the *Mahabharata* during the end of the era Dwapara Yuga mentions a visit of the king Yudhisthira to Sangam in Prayag Raja dating back more than 5,000 years. The religious books *Brahma Purana* and *Kurma Purana* give mention to the importance of this tree. The religious text *Atharva Veda* assumed the tree

Pilgrims at Ardha Kumbh Prayag, Mauni Amavasya (Olaf Rocksien)

Traditional weapons at Kumbh

as *Brahmanda Vriksha*, a tree covering the whole universe from space to sky to the land.

The sacred text of *Matsya Purana* describes the tree of *Akshayawata* as the 'Lord Shiva himself'. Merely the sight of the sacred tree would bring the benefit of salvation to the Hindus. The local priests' and the boatmen's narrations about the immortal Akshayawata tree are beyond ones belief. The tree is deep rooted in the nether world called the seven Patals. The leaves of the tree neither fall nor turn dry. The tree is still peeping from the walls of the Fort where a *Nara Bali* (human sacrifice) of a Brahmin priest was made to encircle the sacred tree into the boundary walls of the fort by the Muslim emperor Akbar. The *Nara Bali* was made near the Begum Gate of the fort facing the river. The Akshyawata tree is identified in the religious text, *Padma Purana*, as located on the north bank of the river Yamuna and on the eastern bank of the river Ganga. It further identifies the place of the holy bath as the river confluence where the streams follow its direction towards the west. The *Matsya Purana* refers to the immortality of the tree when the twelve solar powers in the

Sadhu at rest

universe (*Dwadasha Aaditya*) destroy the entire universe, leaving only the Akshayawata tree at Prayag remaining.

The sacred tree as per the diary of travellers

We find documentary references from eye-witnesses up untill the 16th century as to the existence of a banyan tree growing at the Sangam, north of the river Yamuna. Although it was a new branch, the original tree referred to by the sage Maharishi Valmiki in the Ramayana existed somewhere to the south of the river Yamuna. He named it the *Shyama Vriksha* (the black tree) dating back to the Dwarpa Yuga of the Hindus, approximately 2.5 million years back. In a controversial diary, Huen't' Sang, a Chinese traveller who visited the holy city of Prayag with King Harshwardhana in

644 A.D., recorded the existence of the immortal banyan tree of heaven, the *Akshayawata*. He talks about the importance of a suicide by falling down from the tree. He referred to the bones collected in the left and right hand sides of the holy tree, yet he did not witness a single person attempting suicide in search of salvation. He also referred to a man-eating demon on the tree causing the bone collection on both sides of the tree. He appears to exaggerate and degrade the place. His story of demons and suicide appears contradictory except for Alberuni, who visited the city of Prayag in the 11th century. He wrote about a giant tree at the confluence of the rivers where Brahmins and Kshhatriyas attempted to commit suicide by throwing themselves into the river Ganga. Other authors like Rashiuddin

Kumbh Mela and the Sadhus

(14th century) and Abul Fazal (16th century) documented the existence of the banyan tree at the bank beneath which the stream of Ganga flowed.

Flags at Kumbh

The holy tree trapped inside the fort

Akshayawata was seen by tourists and authors during the late 15th century. The Muslim ruler Akbar hid the Akshayawata within the boundary walls of his fort in the 16th century, acknowledging the fact that the Hindu pilgrims all expressed their faith in the sacred tree and in the land surrounding the tree at the river bank. Abul Fazal, a historian of the time also recorded his findings regarding the tree. Akbar captured the holy tree then later made a sacrificial killing of a Hindu Brahmin and two elephants at the basement while laying the foundation of the fort to make it permanent on the Ganga and Yamuna bed. It is recorded that prior to the human sacrifice buried beneath the fort wall, the foundation was repeatedly washed away by the waves of the river Yamuna.

Sadhu with rifle

The basement with the human sacrifice was extended to capture the Ganga and Yamuna bed at Sangam in an area of 2633 metres in length and 1286 metres in radius.

The Afghan and Muslim invaders and rulers in India aimed at the Akshayawata at Prayag for their communal reasons. A reference to a Naga Gosai Giri fighting with the invaders during the reign of Ahamad Shah shows that Akshayawata was about to fall into the hands of the Afghans in 1751. *Vividha Tirtha Kalpa,* the religious book,

made reference that the tree repeatedly re-developed every time the invading Muslim rulers attempted to cut and destroy it.

Patalpuri Temple and Akshayawata Tree

The immortal tree Akshayawata had been a source of income for the priests and *Tirtha-Purohits* called the *Prayagwalas* from times immemorial. The priests made massive attempts for the release of the trapped Akshayawata. They made several calls for entry of Hindu pilgrims at the site and for permission to let them worship the tree and make charity.

At a location inside the fort from the east-north side, the pilgrims visit an underground area in which they find the enclosure of Patalpuri Temple based on 100 pillars. The paved area, in a length of 25 metres, width of 15.5 metres and height of 2 metres, contains about forty-three full-size shrines made of black marble. The images and shrines were once sealed underground by the ruler Jahangira and were re-opened at a later period.

The pilgrims now find a dry trunk here like a branch cut from the tree of heaven in the paved area. It appears draped in a red cloth with green leaves affixed to it. The Hindus worship the artificially installed trunk as Akshayawata believing that they secure a place in heaven. Devotees offer food grains and coins here as a sacrifice. Even after attainment of India's freedom in 1947, a Hindu pilgrim is not allowed to worship the original Akshayawata tree, which is considered to be the holiest of all.

After careful research, Pt. S. N. Katju of Vishwa Hindu Parishada in the 1940s and 50s, found some remnants of an ancient Bargada (Banyan) tree above the ground with a curved mark like the lotus flower apparently affixed by some Hindu worker who had left it to show the place where the green shoot of Akshayawata remained.

As seen from the river, the tree is spread to a respectable size. However, the pilgrims are still barred from worshiping the main shoot or tying a sacred thread around it and making a Parikrama.

With the belief that this undying tree will survive till the end of the world, the Hindu priests, leaders and the Prayagwalas raised their demand to release the main Akshayawata shoot, trapped inside the boundary walls of Allahabad Fort, for religious rituals like circumambulation, *Pheri,* and encircling the tree with the sacred thread on a religious occasion. During the great bathing fairs of the Kumbh, such calls appeared in the newspapers. Patalpuri Temple is located within the limits of the temporary city called Kumbh Nagar.

Years of Past and Forthcoming Kumbh

Kumbh Haridwar	Kumbh Prayag	Kumbh Nasik	Kumbh Ujjain	Ardha Kumbh Prayag
1253-	1285	—	—	—
1389	—	—	—	—
—	1514	—	—	—
1621	—	—	—	—
1628	—	—	—	—
1640	—	1690	1702	—
—	—	1714	1732	—
—	—	—	1743	—
1748	1751	1754	1755	—
1760	1763	1766	1767	—
1772	1775	1778	1779	—
1784	1787	1790	1790	—
1796	1799	1802	1802	—
1808	1811	1813	1814	—
1819	1822	1825	1826	—
1832	1834	1837	1838	1840
1844	1846	1849	1850	1852
1855	1858	1861	1861	1864
1967	1870	1972	1873	1876
1879	1882	—	1885	1888
1892	1894	1896	1897	1900
1903	1906	—	1909	1912
1915	1918	—	1921	1924
1927	1930	1932	1933	1936
1938	1942	1944	1945	1948
1950	1954	1956	1956-57	1959
1962	1965-66	1968	1968-69	1971
1974	1977	1980	1980	1982
1986	1989	1991	1992	1995
1998	2001	2003	2004	2007
2010	2012	2015	2016	2018
2021	2024	2027	2028	2030
2033	2036	2039	2040	2042

Kumbh Mela and the Sadhus

Major Events at Past Kumbhs

1253 AD	Kumbh Haridwar.	Fighting between Naga Sanyasis and Vaishnawa Sadhus.
1285	Kumbh Trayambak	Nazim visited Kumbh
1389	Maha Kumbh Haridwar	Amir Zafer Taimur looted Mayapuri at Haridwar
1514	Kumbh Prayag	Chaitanya Maha Prabhu visited Prayag Kumbh
1621	Ardha Kumbh Haridwar	Emperor Jahangir observed killing and fighting between Udasi and Vairagies
1640	Kumbh Haridwar	Fighting between the Mundis (Vairagis) and Sanyasis (Naga)
1650	Kumbh Haridwar	Naga Sanyasies killed Vairagis
1690	Kumbh Ujjain	12000 Vairagies were killed in a fight with Sanyasis
1691	Kumbh Nasik	Fadnawis of Sri Holker Sri Rawaji Balaji Parneker constructed Kushawart tirth
1702	Kumbh Nasik	Honourable Court ordered Bairagi Akharas to bathe in Nasik Ram Kund and the Sanyasi Akhara to bathe in Kushawart
1714	Kumbh Nasik	Naga Sanyasis bathe into Kushawart and Vaishnawas into Ramkund. The tradition is still running
1732	Kumbh Ujjain	Gwalior State started a tradition to invite the Akharas at Kumbh Prayag to visit Ujjain, the state made arrangements for the Sadhus
1751	Kumbh Prayag	Sardar Ahmad Khan looted Allahabad city. Monk Sri Rajendra Giri headed 6000 monks who defended the attack and killings
1760	Kumbh Haridwar	18000 Vairagi sadhus killed in fight with the Naga sanyasis
1796	Kumbh Haridwar	Captain Thomas Hardwick visits Kumbh. 5000 Sadhus were killed by Sikh Army of Patiyala
1808	Kumbh Haridwar	British traveller Felix Winset Raper wrote he never saw such number of pilgrims to bathe at any other place
1819	Kumbh Haridwar	450 pilgrims were killed at Har ki Pauri due to mismanagement
1840	Kumbh Prayag	One Christian observer visited Kumbh
1844	Kumbh Haridwar	Miraculous powers of Baba Shrawan Nath

1846	Kumbh Prayag	Establishment of Udasin Panchayati Naya Akhara
1855	Kumbh Haridwar	Establishment of Nirmal Panchayati Akhara Bala Saheb Peshawa, Tatya Tope and others planned to uproot British Rule from india
1872	Kumbh Nasik	Restriction imposed over naked bathing of Nagas
1876	Ardha Kumbh Prayag	Swami Dayanand introduced Aarya Samaj at Ardh Kumbh
1879	Kumbh Haridwar	Internal dispute amongst the Akharas on the issue to bathe first into the river resulted into killing of 500 Sadhus. The Akharas decided a bathing sequence to be followed.
1882	Kumbh Prayag	Mr. T Baisan, ICS, gave detailed description of Kumbh
1885	Kumbh Ujjain	Internal fight in between the Vaishnawas and Naga Sanyasis resulted in killing and looting. Kumbh Ujjain was boycotted by the Das Nami Shambhu Bhairawa Akhara after the incidence
1892	Kumbh Haridwar	Ban imposed due to Cholera
1896	Kumbh Nasik	Police Act imposed on the Akharas
1906	Kumbh Prayag	Prince and Princess of Wales visited India.s Internal dispute occurred in Vaishnawa Anies
1907	Kumbh Ujjain	Nagas agreed to join Kumbh Ujjain on invitation of the kingly state
1909	Kumbh Haridwar	Mahatma Gandhi visited Kumbh and chalked out the non-cooperation Movement against the British
1921	Kumbh Ujjain	Sri Ramanand Sampradaya and Sri Ramanuja Sampradaya decided to be separate
1927	Kumbh Haridwar	The uncontrolled crowd resulted in stampede and death
1932	Kumbh Nasik	The Nagas were allowed to bathe naked into the river subject to their return before sunrise
1944	Ardha Kumbh Haridwar	The British Government banned Kumbh due to war
1944	Kumbh Nasik	Bathing sequence of the Akharas and order of priority to bathe decided
1950	Kumbh Ujjain	The state denied permission for Mela Arrangement due to war, but the Akharas and the public decided to bear and share the arrangements and celebrated Kumbh

1954		The incidence of Kumbh 1954 happened when a Naga procession of an Akhara on its way back from Sangam could not control its elephant in a massive crowd. The crowd moved uncontrolled due to mismanagement and some sort of *'Lathi charge'* on the Mela ground. It happened upon the arrival of an important person into the Mela area.
1956	Kumbh Ujjain	Difference of opinion on Kumbh date/time between Karpatri Dandi Swami and ShatDarshan Akharas
1959	Ardha Kumbh Prayag	Conflict between Mela administration and Akharas resulted in Boycott of First Shahi Bath. Akhil Bhartiya Shat Darshan Akhara Parishad was organised to solve this problem.
1962	Kumbh Haridwar	Order of merit decided for Shahi Snan for Akharas
1966	Kumbh Prayag	Conflict in Astronomical calculation resulted in two Kumbh Parvas in 1965 and in 1966
1980	Kumbh Ujjain	Conflict over the issues of Akhara tradition
1986	Kumbh Haridwar	The Chief ministers from U.P., Bihar, Haryana visited for a sacred bath at Har ki Pauri. Accident occurred due to blockage of the crowd on main passage.
1989	Kumbh Prayag	Conflict over the post of Ramanandacharya in Vaishnawa Akharas. Conflict over the sequence of Shahi between Juna, Aawahan and Agni Akharas. Conflicts between Vishwa Hindu Parishad and Bharat Sadhu Samaj
1991	Kumbh Nasik	Akhara Parishad objected to declaration for four Shahi Snans by Mela Administration contrary to three bathing events.
1992	Kumbh Ujjain	Rajmata Sindhiya was also invited by the Mela Administration to attend Welcome Ceremony at Kumbh
1995	Ardha Kumbh Prayag	The Akharas boycotted Shahi Snan on Maker Sankranti Day
1998	Kumbh Haridwar	Conflict over the order of bathing sequence
2001	Kumbh Prayag	Remained full of conflicts, Bathing sequence of the Akharas converted into Bathing time by Mela Administration

| 2010 | Kumbh Haridwar | Due to the explosion of a domestic LPG cylinder, a fire broke out in the *Bairagi* camp area leaving one woman dead and injuring more than twelve others. |
| 2010 | Kumbh Haridwar | A stampede near the *Birla Ghat* during the last *Shahi snan* at *Kumbh Mela* Haridwar caused the death of seven persons including one child. This incident took place while the *Shahi* procession of *Mahamandeleshwar* of *Juna Akhara* was proceeding for *Shahi snan*. After the incident, *Juna, Agni* and *Awaahan Akharas* decided to bathe at the *Birla Ghat* instead of bathing at *Brahmakund*. Other *Akharas* took a dip at *Brahmakund*. |

Holy man at Kumbh (Olaf Rocksien)

Kumbh Mela and the Sadhus

Chapter 3
Holy men at Kumbh Prayag

With special reference to Juna Akhara at Kumbh Nagar

When the holy men move out in a *Shahi* procession on the specific bathing days, they form the greatest show of Hindu ascetics on earth. The Sadhu-Sanyasi from Vaishanava and Shaiva sects provide the real colour on specific bathing days. Hindu holy men are not seen staying for a long time at any location, nor do they usually appear unclothed or naked in public. They come out of their Mathas, Aashramas, Akharas, Dhunas, caves, hilltops and the dense forests, etc., to assemble en masse under their sect banners during Kumbh at Haridwar, Prayag, Nasik and Ujjain. Prayag attracts the highest number of holy men in India and is considered 'the holiest converging point of the Hindus'.

The *Hatha Yogis* and Sadhus demonstrating their martial powers draw the attention of the crowds who throng the fair. These holy men have renounced their families and material life and are held in high respect by the Hindu pilgrims. The devotees and the householders often search for a *Siddha* with supernatural powers among the holy men, looking to receive their blessings to fulfil worldly desires and secure a place for themselves in heaven.

Baba Ramdev, Kumbh 2007 (Rama Nand Tiwari)

Kumbh Mela and the Sadhus

Aerial view of Kumbh Nagar

The government's Kumbh Mela Administration invites them to visit the Kumbh by sending a printed invitation then provides arrangements for these holy men during the Mela. The holy men under their Akhara banners are allotted land and other amenities while they join the fair.

The preparation begins before the commencement of the *Mela*. The land surfacing, electrification, sanitation, water supply, vehicle passes and food supplies are made available to the holy men entering into the Mela on a priority basis.

The Akharas at the Kumbh fair house the Sadhus and saints under specific traditions, banners, and sects. They camp for several days or weeks on the sandy land under their flags. Every Akhara in the Mela has its own flag fixed on high poles. Night security is arranged by the Akharas themselves, where the entrance is provided with gates made of bamboo poles. They settle their camps at vantage points away from householders and the Kalpavasis. The main entrance gate of an Akhara in general is opened to the public in the early hours of the morning until late evening, others may keep the entrance gates open for their members throughout the night.

The holy men of the Hindus and their Royal procession the Shahi forms the main attraction at Kumbh when the naked ascetics move out of their Akharas. The Shahi Snana, or the procession of religious baths, was availed by 13 Akharas during Kumbh Prayag 1989, whereas 55 Akharas had their presence in the Mela area. 37 Mandaleshwaras and 17 Maha Mandaleshwaras, including the Jagat-Gurus of Shaiva and Vaishanava Sects, camped in the Mela as religious heads. The Jagat-Gurus, the teachers of the universe, are the highest in the religious cadre. Their rank included the Ramanandacharya, the Ramanujacharya and four Shankaracharyas who visited the Kumbh Mela in 1989.

Warrior Saints at Kumbh

The entrance of the religious heads into the Mela is another major attraction to the devotees. They move through in Gold and Silver chariots, holding *Palki, Sawari, Chhatra, Chhanwara, Dhwaja, and Haudas* on the backs of elephants and horses. An accompanying band follows along forming large processions.

There is a welcome ceremony known as *Agawani* on their entrance into the Mela area. At Kumbh 1954, a Naga procession of an Akhara returning from Sangam could not control its elephant. There was some sort of Lathi charge on the Mela ground, an important person arrived into the area and the massive crowd moved uncontrolled due to mismanagement.

Among the the Sadhus, the Naga Sadhu and Sanyasi appear as 'the holiest holy men of the Hindus,' around whom the attention of the devotees and observers revolves. Naga ascetics are recognised for their quick anger, aggressive militancy and rigidity on certain issues.

Female Monks in Shahi procession

The Sector Five camp of the Juna Akhara Sanyasis during Kumbh Prayag 2001, was called Akhara Cobra by the Police authorities. The Ash smeared Sadhus, whether "skyclad" or clad in ochre robes, lion cloth or a lion skin, outnumber the laity at the Mela. The Juna Akhara claimed to house more than one lac (1,00,000) ascetics under their banner.

The Nagas have taken precedence over the bathing arrangements during the Kumbh since its conception. No sooner does the *Parva* start than they avail their order of priority at the Sangam. They march out naked with their specific Akharas to join the procession. The main bathing point at the bathing ghat (known as the Sangam Nose) is vacated by the Hindu householders (*grihasthas*) until the holy men have completed their bath on specific Mela days.

Mela Pandal at Kumbh

The 5th and 11th of December 2000

The Sadhus, Sanyasi, Saints, Holy men and Ascetics were about to assemble at *Kumbh Nagar,* a temporary city at Allahabad during the first Maha Kumbh fair of the century. It was a distance of about 120 kilometres from the holy city of Varanasi. The temperature was moderate, time about 10 a.m. The land was the sandy bed of the holy rivers Ganga and Yamuna at the North East axis of the confluence. Massive work was going on to convert the unequal sandy bed into a temporary city—Kumbh Nagar.

Moving back towards the east about two kilometres, the level of the land was totally uneven, sloppy and unfit for an open sky camping facility. This location, a short distance from the river confluence, was reserved for the religious Akharas whom the Mela administration had invited. About 22 tractors were engaged by the Mela administration for levelling the land, installation of electric poles and chequered plates, etc.

The chequered plate roads connected the land with a pontoon bridge over the river Ganga, facilitating movement towards the south-east bank of the river. The permanent concrete road called *Kali Saraka* extended along the north east bank of the river towards the Mela administration office and Daraganj locality. The sandy bed was also divided in *Ganga*

Painting by BD Pandey

Dweepa and *Yamuna Dweepa* meaning islands of the rivers Ganga and Yamuna. There were no camping facilities yet on the sandy bed, hence the holy-men of Juna Akhara camped temporarily to the south of *Kali Saraka,* the black road. Their resting place was beneath an old Peepal tree surrounded by temples at a short distance from the Mela office. The location had a *Dhuni,* the sacred fire pit. The group of Akhara secretaries had settled here to look after the camping facilities on the sand before the entry of the Akhara procession into the Mela area.

Rituals of Dhwaja Rohana and Bhumi Pujan

Sri Panch Das Naam Juna Akhara had taken a huge area of open land at the Kumbh Prayag to house the visiting Sanyasis at Kumbh. The concerned secretaries of the Akhara had estimated the requirement of tented houses for the incoming holy men. It was surprising they were able to estimate this in the absence of a documentary record of the Naga hermitages attached to the Akhara. About one thousand holy men of Juna Akhara were present on the sandy land, some clothed in saffron, some naked, having huge bundles of matted hair on their head—*Jata.* The first rituals of the holy men began with *Dhwajarohana* and *Bhumi Pujana* meaning affixing the flag and worship of the land. The Sanyasis present here had come from different corners of the country. The female Sanyasis, the *Nagin*, belonged to the capital of India, Delhi, and to neighbouring Nepal.

At a distance of about fifty metres from the road, inside the boundary limits of Juna Akhara, there was a platform about two feet high, which the holy-men had constructed the previous days. A square shaped sacred fire pit called *Yagya Kunda* was made on a high platform for worship rituals. It was surrounded by fruit, flowers, colours, vegetables, cloth and cereals. To the right of the platform they dug a pit about eleven feet deep with a circumference of about seven feet in the shape of an *Argha* of a *Shiva Lingama*, the narrow end facing the South-East. The pit was dug to the North -East of the place called *Ishana Kona*. As a rule, the *Garbha Griha,* inner sanctum formation, the Deity and the flag of the Akhara, are to be located in the North -East corner. A full length tree, lower diameter two feet, was pulled near the pit. The holy men were now all busy.

The tree was painted saffron colour, with a sacred thread on the upper end, tied into a number of fifty-two circular knots which denotes fifty-two *Madhies* (recruitment centres) attached to Juna Akhara. The figure fifty-two denoted a symbolic representation of the Akhara many ways. The length of the pole above the ground was about fifty-two *Hatha* (Hands). The diameter of the triangular arms of the Akhara flag was also about fifty-two *Hatha*, approximately twenty-six yards. We found another connection to the number fifty-two in the *Dhawaja Rohana Samroha* ceremony when the saints moved towards Aawahan and Agni Akharas followed by a visit to Alakha Durbar. That ceremony ended at the mother's hermitage Mai-Bara where the male Naga Sanyasi monks were not allowed.

Here the holy-men opened a saffron flag, held it above the ground, and shouted loudly *Dutta Maharja Ki Jai, Har-Har Mahadeva* meaning a victory to the supreme king Dattatreya and Lord Shiva the supreme God. The flag was tied to the upper end of the pole. The base of the flag perpendicular to the pole formed a large hand. The base of the pole was further tied with a coconut rope from top to middle at four different points. The holy men were divided into five groups to fix the flag pole into the pit and tie the ropes to the surface. They placed a few coins, fruits and flowers into the pit as a sacrifice to make the flag stable until the end of the Kumbh celebrations.

Entry of the Pilgrims

The Sanyasi group held the flag in their hands, affixed the flag base into the pit by tying the ropes in four directions to the ground giving criss-cross support to the poles. The flag was now flying high in the sky. The Sanyasis of the Akhara were then divided into four different groups according their specific Madhi name and group order combinations. Jointly they held the Akhara flag in their attempt to affix the ropes to the ground.

The Akhara flag fixed to territorial land was a static deity symbolizing the Supreme Power. Just below the Akhara flag, a Kalasha (pot) was kept. It was filled with the sacred water of the river Ganga from where Varuna, the God of Water, was invited to attend the Kumbh at the Akhara grounds. The Kalasha was made of mud. On the outer surface barley grains were affixed to grow into herbs and appear green till the end of the Mela. With day's end today started a period of seven days for the holy men

Juna Akhara Monks making their entry at Kumbh

to complete their preparations of the residential accommodations, amenities and fire pit (Dhuna) at the Akhara grounds.

December 28th 2000

The entrance gate of the Akhara with its banner was ready. The outer boundary of the Akhara land was encircled with bamboo strips. The Sanyasis under Madhi groups were further sub-divided into family orders, based on the seat of their religious teachers or Guru. They were busy in erecting the individual tented houses on the sandy bed. People selling cloth, carpets,

Juna Akhara Monks making their entry at Kumbh

blankets, Rudraksha beads, plastic sheets and mats (*chatai*), and some physical labourers entered into the Akhara campus at midday to provide the necessary materials to establish the camp.

Dry grass and wooden log vendors were moving on elephants. The high platform beneath the Akhara flag was encircled and barricaded with bamboo poles and strips. It formed a worship place as a seat of the chief deity, known as *Gadi* or *Gaddi*. The platform of the main deity's Gadi had a symbolic footprint of the supreme teacher, which the monks called the *Charana Paduka* of Guru Maharaja. Similar to their chief deity Guru, the holy men had settled pictures of their own family Guru, along with idols of other deities and Gods, in front of their camping tents.

The evening time was a busy hour for the Akhara secretaries and

Niranjani Akhara Monks making their entry at Kumbh

authorities for they had many problems to solve. (1) To link with the Mela Administration, (2) To allocate different tasks among the secretaries, (3) To make a link with the Press and Media, (4) To watch any humour and doubtful activity, (5) To avail a vehicle pass to facilitate the lodging and

Niranjani Akhara at Kumbh

food facilities, (6) To attend the invitations from religious heads, (7) To attend the meetings of Akhara Parishada, (8) To invite a meeting of Akhara secretaries on any urgent issue, (9) To attend a salutation of the fellow ascetics at prayer time, (10) To make strategies for the coming Shahi procession and Sahibi election, (11) To perform daily penances, Yoga and worship, etc.

Today was Niranjani Akhara's turn to celebrate Dhwaja Rohana. A few other saints were about to enter into the Mela area with a traditional procession. We decided to visit some saints at Juna Akhara who had settled their camp seats, their *Gaddies*.

Mahanta Haridwar Giri of 13 Madhi, belonging to the Kapoorthala family, Ambawala Dera, Punjab, had settled to the east corner of the Akhara. A Naga ascetic of bold physical appearance, Mahanta Haridwar Giri always appeared leading the Akhara deity in Shahi processions. His camp opened onto another lane at the rear of the Akhara. At about 4 p.m. just after the Dhwaja Rohana of Niranjani Akhara, his Guruji visited his *Gaddi* which had been decorated with a new carpet. Mahanta Haridwar Giri paid

Religious heads of Juna Akhara at Kumbh Prayag

respect to his Guru as per tradition. Guruji having joined his seat was offered an evening meal along with the visitors. We also joined the Pangata, where Mahanta Giri, as a token of an after meal gift, offered a cash gift Dakshina to all those who attended. Next we visited Sri Mahanta Parm Nanda Saraswati, who camped just right of the Gadi of the Akhara deity. The Naga ascetic aged about 60 years, a singularly featured and active holy man with free movement of his body, having his Aashrama in Tata Jamshedpur, Jharkhand, was a public relations officer or an Akhara spokesman, later elected as the president of the Akhara. The chief secretary to the Government of U.P., the Mela commissioner, and the Mela S.S.P. visited Sri Mahanta Parmnanda Saraswati at Juna Akhara in his camp.

There were the Pandals (tents) of the religious organisations and the monks like Vishwa Hindu Parishad, the Yogi and Tantrika ascetics. Some Pandals displayed, on their entrance gates, the life size picture of a saint who was still alive. Entry of a common pilgrim to visit the saint was restricted in most of the centres. The crowd passing by outside would peep into the Pandals to just view the comfortable and luxurious seats of the religious heads, their colourful carpets, lion skin or deer skin and would pay regard to the possessions.

Religious Processions at Kumbh

The entire Mela area was completely alive this day for the inflow of pilgrims was increasing. The crowd had several entry points from Jhunsi, Daraganj, Bairahana and Bandh localities. The casual visitors, who would stay only a day or two, were coming in groups on foot with luggage on their heads. The incoming pilgrims followed the paths on which they visited Kumbh Mela in the past. They rested here and there under the open sky at the riverbank where a few other families had already settled. They made pits in the sand to cook food. During such halts, the housewives would prepare a meal while the male members would rest in the open, completely unconcerned for any theft or loss. They liked to stay at a short distance from the river stream or other water source. Among the devotee's goals were Sangam bathing, visits to Patalpuri Temple, Akshayawata (the holy tree) and Parikrama (circumambulation) of the holy land. They also would not miss visiting the saints and Mahatmas present in an Akhara or elsewhere.

The Deity of Juna Akhara enters the Mela area

Two divisions of the Akhara administration, (i) the static and (ii) the roaming groups, had deities to be carried to Kumbh Mela grounds. On specific Mela days, the deity leads the Shahi procession and takes the first dip into the sacred river water.

The Naga Sanyasis of Juna Akhara had completed laying the foundation for the Akhara flag, the *Varuna Kalasha* (water pot) and the platform for *Charana Paduka* (holy feet). To the rear, they prepared a storeroom, called a *Kothara*, which was a secured place with a restricted entry.

Their mobile Akhara Deity, *Dewata*, also called *Nisana*, was in the form of long iron spears called *Bhala*. The Varanasi Head office of Juna Akhara worships Bhala daily. A small group of Naga ascetics, the Dewata Panch, carried the deity a distance of about 140 kilometres from Varanasi to Allahabad. They completed the journey on foot within a period of five days, halting at five places. The senior ascetics of Buddha Panch settled into the Mela area received and greeted the Dewata Panch.

One householder priest, who stayed somewhere in a temple on

Juna Akhara Monks at Kumbh

the east side of the sandy bed approaching the Jhunsi Road, joined today's ritual with a unit of approximately fifteen Naga ascetics. The group entered with the Akhara deity into the Kumbh Nagar Mela area before night.

Feeding the monks at Kumbh

There were two ascetics who held the Bhala on their shoulders. The long iron spears as deities were decorated with flowers, *Churi* and *Kangana* (bracelets) and *Rori* (a red powder). The Naga monks carrying the spear deities were bare-footed and semi nude, wearing only a Langoti (loin cloth). From one side of the riverbed they crossed a pontoon bridge to reach the locality of Dasaswamedh Ghat at Daraganj. This area was overcrowded with devotees and vegetable sellers on the road.

The senior Naga monks of the Buddha Panch at Kumbh Mela welcomed the ascetics of the Dewata Panch and garlanded the Dewata deity. As a security arrangement, the local police escorted the procession from Daraganj to reach Alopi Bagh Temple. One of the groups carrying the Akhara Deity stayed inside the campus of the temple and another group stayed outside with their Deity. The Dewata left here belonged to Aawahan Akhara. From this place the Naga ascetics of Aawahan Akhara followed the Kafila of Juna Akhara. The ascetics joined the road route towards Naini Bridge on the river Yamuna. They brought the Dewata to Mauj Giri Aashrama and stayed there for the next ritual.

The monks appeared busy everywhere as some sort of Mela activities were going on in almost every Akhara. The roads on the way at Malviya Bridge and Bundh side were jammed with onlookers.

January 7th 2001 Call for lunch and dinner in Akhara

The Naga saints had individual fire pits (*Dhuni*) in front of their resting camps. As a rule a Sanyasi normally does not ignite a fire or cook food, yet here at Kumbh it is an exception. The flame of the sacred Dhunis protect the naked saints from the chilling cold and is also used to prepare tea, etc. There are separate kitchens under their Madhi groups for group meals. We had the opportunity to join a common dinner assembly inside the Akhara as householder devotees on three successive Kumbh occasions. There were approximately five householders to cook the food. The work serving the prepared food was performed by the Naga ascetics. One had to take his shoes off outside the entrance gate of the kitchen before joining the meal assembly sitting on a long carpet.

The kitchen in-charge might wear a saffron cloth or be smeared with ashes. A Naga monk served the meal and called out for every item he served. The specific call was Maharaja Bhojana Ki Hari Hara meaning, O supreme king, join the food assembly in the name of the deity Vishnu and Shiva.

Alakh Sanayasis of Juna Akhara

They suffixed the name of the Lord Rama to the names of the food, i.e. Jala-Rama (drinking water), Roti-Rama (bread), Dala-Rama (cooked pulses), Sabji-Rama (Vegetables), Rama-Rasa (Salt) etc. The naked monk ascetics in Digambara who smear their body

Kumbh Mela and the Sadhus

with ashes would sit as usual. Householder and women devotees could join the meal sitting at a distance from the Naga ascetics' row.

The ritual of Chhawani Prawesh
(Entry into the Cantonment Area)
Juna Akhara, Kumbh Allahabad; January 7, 2001

The entry of the Holy-men into the Cantonment Area is called *Peshawai* or *Chhawani Pravesh*. It is connected with the tradition of the Indian ruling states of the past to invite them to visit Kumbh fairs and follows a ritual tradition. The wandering Naga ascetics are warrior saints who appear to penetrate into an area under a call for help or by force. The Mela administration of the government now invites and welcomes the ascetics and saints who ritually declare their entry into the Mela area.

The presence of different ascetic Akharas at the Kumbh fairs, signifies one of the oldest religious traditions in India. It is said that in the past the Naga Sanyasis accompanied the Shahi of the elevated religious heads who were entitled to hold the signs and symbols of a king. Hence, there follows the tradition to royally welcome the incoming religious heads who would lead the Shahi, the sacred bathing procession at Kumbh.

Today, the mobile units of Juna Akhara Ramata Panch and Dewata Panch combined together at the outer limits of Kumbh Nagar near Naini Bridge. At about 8 a.m. the monks moved for Mauj Giri Ashram, where they witnessed a presence of about five thousand Naga ascetics, male and female, some naked or some wearing saffron cloth. The Naga ascetics of Buddha Panch greeted and welcomed the ascetics of the Ramata Panch inside their tented camps and seats.

The procession of the monks started at 10 a.m. and extended to a length of one kilometre. The Naga Sanyasis put on a big show on the road followed by *Lingi Kriya* as a part of their 'Hatha Yoga' practices. They would roll up their *Linga* (male genital sex organ), on the rod of a *Trishul*, Shiva's trident, and hold a load of one or two monks on either ends of the horizontal bar. Next was to pull a police patrolling jeep with the *Lingam*. The vehicle was attached to the bar, using a long cloth as a rope. With the car tied to his linga bar and hand held, the sadhu then pulled the vehicle on the road without any other device. It was 4 p.m. when the *Julus* (procession) of *Peshawai* reached *Lal Sarak* (red coloured road), extending to a length of four kilometres. The weather was too hot to easily quench one's thirst. The road on both sides was overcrowded at every point. Reaching in front of Mela administration Camp, the office bearers of the Akhara were welcomed by Mela S.S.P. as an essential act of Agawani for Peshawai Julus. However, the other administrative authorities did not appear to welcome them, which the monks considered an insult. The procession now reached Sector Five where the monks and the saints of other Akharas came out to welcome Juna Akhara.

Monk performing Linga Kriya

Akhara elephant Shiva Gaja could not enter into Kumbh Nagar for the Mela administration had restricted its entry into the Mela area as a precaution after the 1954 Kumbh incident. The last were the Palkies of the senior and head monks, the Aacharya MahaMandaleshwar of Juna Akhara, Shri Awadheshnanda Giri and a few others including a lady ascetic. The Sanyasis who accompanied the Peshwai were now paying salutations to the Akhara flag in a formal posture. Next was the *Danka - Dana* ritual on a high platform beneath the *(Akhara Dhwaja)* Akhara Flag at the *Charana Paduka* of Guru Maharaja.

The Aacharya Mahamandeleshwara of Juna Akhara who moved for the *'Danka Dana'* ceremony was busy with the media and the monks. The negligence of the Mela administration authorities in not welcoming the Peshwai (entry) procession of the different Akharas provoked the Sanyasi monks to express anger.

"I believe in God, who reveals himself in the orderly harmony of the universe, and I believe that intelligence is manifested throughout mother nature." - Albert Einstein

After their entry inside the Akhara, the chief monks came out of the *Palkies* (palanquins) and moved to worship the *Charan-Paduka* (silver footprints) of the supreme teacher Sri Guru Maharaja. As per ritual, the monks joining the procession on a Palki made sacrificial donations in cash. The Akhara secretary announced donations in a high-pitched voice followed by a double drum beat. The announcement versed *Sri Panch Das Naam, Om Guru Murtiyo Sunana ji Sri... ne. Sri Guru ji Maharaja Ko. Rupaye Bhet Puja mien diya.* It is brought to the witness of all the members that Sri ... (Name) ...of... (Place) ... donated a sum of Rupees ... (amount) as a token of worship and gift to Sri Guruji Maharaja.

As a routine of daily worship in the evening the Naga Sanyasi beat a drum and rang a bell hanging on a wooden post support to sound loudly near the platform of *Danka Daan.*

January 13th 2001. Juna Akhara at Kumbh Allahabad

The Akhara atmosphere was full of chaos and activities from early morning. The Akhara area was open to casual visitors and devotees. We received a breakfast of *Pakaudi* and *Halawa* at 7 a.m. at the camp of Sri Mahanta Parmananda Saraswati. The saints had prepared for them *'Bhang Ki Pakaudi'* an intoxicating item made from Ganja. Daily milk consumption for tea, etc., was approximately one quintal or 1000 litres in one Madhi group with food preparation for approximately 2000 persons. The foods were Basmati rice, Desi Ghee (clarified butter), pickles, roti (bread), etc. The Akhara recorded the presence of about fifteen thousand Nagas whereas the total number of saints throughout India was said to be about one lakh fifty thousand. Today the Dhunis of the saints were visited by the priests of the Naga monks called the *Jangama* and *Alakha*. Both groups are monks associated with Das Naam Naga Sanyasis.

The Jangams could be recognised as the Sadhus wearing saffron cloth, earrings and a cap on the head with peacock feathers, fixed with one white circular medal of approximately two inches in diameter. They carry ringing bells in their hands and cover their heads with a red canopy.

While visiting in groups of nine to ten at a Dhuni, their job was to sing the songs of the Das Naam family and to please the naked ascetics. In token they would receive gifts and donations. The songs they recited were a hereditary transfer of the oral records which might continue for eight hours or more. While singing they shook their heads and bells

Jangam Sanayasis of Juna Akhara

alike. The Jangams are householder Sadhus who keep family ties. They appear at Kumbh coming from Haryana.

The Jangams are associated with the story of Lord Shiva's marriage ceremony. After the wedding of Lord Shiva, Lords Bramha and Vishnu approached him to offer gifts as Daana and Dakshina. But Lord Shiva refused to accept the gifts and slapped his *Jangha* (thigh) creating the Jangams who accepted the gifts for him, thus finalizing his marriage ceremony. Following the mythological story, the Jangams wander from one Naga Dhuni to another to receive gifts and alms.

The Alakha are entitled to accept alms and donations from ten named orders of Naga monks. The unique feature of the Alakhas is that, with their legs, they ring bells which hang down from their waist. The rhythm of ringing bells does not stop nor do they wait for a long time standing at any particular place to beg alms. They always carry a horizontal vessel called a *Khappada* to collect gifts and accept offerings of the alms. Alakhas shake their legs continuously to ring the bells whereas the Jangams shake their head and hands to ring the bells.

The Alakha, while visiting and ringing, would carry a bag hanging from the shoulders to collect alms. As a rule, they neither sit nor move back to

Naga monks at Juna Akhara

accept alms whereas Jangams would sit to accept alms. The Alakhas generally moved in groups of six to seven. They settled their camp at Alakha Durabara to the East and rear of Juna Akhara.

An Alakha Sanyasi is recognised by his peculiar way of wearing a saffron coloured cloth tied above his waist with cloth-belts approximately three inches in breadth. He carries a *Chanwara* made of peacock feathers, ashes in *Khappada*, waist tied with a rosary of Rudraksha beads, bag and bells hanging to waist front. I found the Nagas ready with their alms and offerings to donate to the members of Alakha Durbar outside their camps facing around their Dhuni fire pits.

Naga monks at Juna Akhara

The pilgrim crowd wandered from one naked ascetic to another. They showed no interest in the senior monks appearing in saffron clothes, although these senior Naga monks had earlier subjected their bodies to physical penance such as living naked and smeared with ashes, after which they were entitled to wear the saffron cloth.

Renunciation of ties and acceptance of Sanyas by the householders. The supreme sacrifice on earth.

It happened late evening time on 13 January, 2001, the night before the first bathing ceremony of holy Kumbh. The scene outside the Akhara premises was building intensity. The road, which had appeared to be an empty sandy bed a few days ago, was now converted into a crowded land flowing with newly arriving pilgrims.

The president of Juna Akhara was in a hurry to exit the Mela camping area in his Toyota 4-wheeler to receive a householder couple. It was next to impossible to move through the location due to a continuous rush of pilgrims inflating Kumbh Nagar. Exiting from the area, we found the couple with imported cars. The couple along with their son and driver, on arrival at Juna Akhara greeted the Naga monk, Sri Mahanta Parmananda Saraswati, with a bouquet of flowers. The aspirants, a young couple, were a man in a suit and a married woman in a saree, shawl and make-up. Belonging to a rich family of Delhi running a large scaled fruit business, the multi-millionaire householders had made up their minds to accept Brahmacharya and enter

into a Sanyas life, leaving behind their worldly possessions and family ties. Sri Mahanta Parmnanda Saraswati, the Akhara President, was their teacher the Sanyas Guru. "We decided to adopt monks lives at Juna Akhara following the Shaivatic sect because it is a leading sect", said the newcomer couple. The young lady in her woollen shawl further narrated that they were asked to finish all their responsibilities with family ties before they came back to join the Akhara and that she had left all worldly possessions. The

The householders leave worldly affairs

young couple had to undergo sacred Akhara rituals to accept the fourth order of Sanyas Aashrama, which was to be held on 14th January, 2001.

Female monks of Juna Akhara at Kumbh Prayag

Juna Akhara accepts ladies to be initiated as female monks at Kumbh Prayag who are called *Mai* and titled the *Nagin*. There is a separate enclosure *Mai Bara* or mother's hermitage for the female monks to stay with their teacher during Kumbh and Ardha Kumbh, opposite to the main entrance gate of Juna Akhara. Those who receive a Sanskara as a *Lingi Kriya* under the religious flag *Dharma Dhwaja* other than an initiation under *Virja Hawan Diksha* would stay in separate camps other than the Mai Bara. The lady monks, *Mais* or the *Nagin* do not appear to hold a portfolio in the main elected executive body of the Akhara. But they are awarded the title of a *Sri Mahanta* for a particular zone or area to which one belongs. They would move out on decorated Palanquins in Shahi and

attend a Danka Daana beneath their religious flag. Yet the rites pertaining to the female ascetics are performed inside the tented houses, where no outsider or male member could enter. The female novitiates wear an uncut piece of cloth called a *Ganti* and assemble beneath the Akhara Flag around the flames of the fire pit at four different corners of their Madhi groups prior to their transformation as a monk.

Sri Mata Anandmayi Ma

Chapter 4
Bathing Days at Kumbh

Makar Sankranti, Mauni Amavasya and Basant Panchami

Shahi at Kumbh Prayag, 14 January, 2010

The festive Akhara atmosphere awakened everyone at 5 a.m. For the Sadhus, it was the day of the first Shahi procession to a holy bath. The lavatory was over-crowded. Householders were not allowed to enter the latrines made for the ascetics. Everyone was taking a bath in an open field where it was freezing cold. The Nagas after bathing smeared their bodies with ashes. In every direction the Nagas were engaged in this routine. At about 6 a.m., Mahanta Muktananda Saraswati issued us a pass to join the Shahi as an *Akhara Sewaka* (servant and devotee of the Akhara). Similarly the cloth wearing Naga Sanyasis put Akhara badges on their chests. About 6:30 a.m., the religious head Jagadguru Shankaracharya associated with Juna Akhara entered with his disciples from the east side of the Akhara.

Monks by Dhuna

Kumbh Mela and the Sadhus

Juna Akhara Preparing for Shahi

He joined the V.I.P. camp of Juna Akhara whereas the devotees following him stayed outside with a saffron flag in their hands. Entry into the Akhara from the main gate was now restricted. The householders were made to leave the Akhara boundaries, as they were not allowed to move with the naked ascetics in Shahi. The time schedule for the procession to move out was 7 a.m. The tractors converted into *Rathas* came out of the Akhara.

At about 6.45 a.m., the Akhara atmosphere was noisy. The naked saints smearing ashes on their bodies came out of their camps forming a queue.

Preparing for Shahi

They appeared naked, wearing a garland of marigold flowers crosswise; some decorated their matted hair with the flowers. The Nagas, who were settled in four directions of the Akhara flag, formed four separate lines up to the main entrance gate. The swelling crowd of naked monks pushed one another attempting to move out. The physical show of human power appeared like a wave of boiling water as they started jumping with

72

their swords, *lathi, trishul, chimta* and other weapons. Crying *Har-Har Mahadev* with full strength they were trying to come out on the road yet the senior monks wearing a *Ganti* commanded the troops. No one other than the senior Naga monks could move with the naked ascetics in the Shahi procession. The Jangams moved separately to the Naga's queue and the Alakhs did not appear in their traditional cloth. At about 6:50 a.m., some physically bold Nagas came out carrying the Dewata, the deity in the form of a long spear decorated with flowers, bangles, and *janeau* (sacred thread) and carried on the shoulder by a Naga. A group of Naga saints covered the deity as bodyguards as one householder Brahmin priest accompanied them. One of the ascetics carried rice grains in his hands which he sprinkled on the ground while murmuring sacred Mantras.

Leaving for Shahi

The Shahi moved out on the road at 7 a.m. sharp. A band playing religious songs led the procession. The mobile Akhara flag fixed to a small non-motorised vehicle pulled by the householders followed the Drumbeater ascetics on horse.

One naked Naga beat two drums. Then the group of about one hundred

Mass bathing at Kumbh

Nagas, who had covered the spear-shaped Akhara Dewata as bodyguards, moved and another group came out carrying Guru Maharaja Ki Palaki on their shoulders. The Palaki was a silver seat in a mini temple structure carrying the *Khadau*, a wooden shoe of the supreme teacher. The naked Nagas followed the deity. This was followed by twin chariots of the great saints, the Shankaracharya and the Maha Mandaleshwara, side by side. Other Palakies of the saints like Pilot Baba and a woman ascetic joined the procession. At the end were the lady monks and the Nagins who wore Ganti and smeared their body with ashes. A moment later the deities moved out, Danka, Nisana, Dewata, Dhwaja, Palki, and the Aacharya of Aawahana and Agni Akharas joined the Shahi with Juna.

The Shahi quickly covered a distance of about 100 metres. The procession moved in the following order (1) First in sequence, the Danka, Nisana and Dewata of Juna with Aawahan Akharas moved jointly in a horizontal appearance as equals, leading the Shahi. Aawahan Akhara did not join Juna at this time. (2) Second was the Dhwaja (flag) and the Palki of Juna Akhara deity, followed by the Dhwaja and Palki of Aawahan

Mass bathing at Kumbh

Akhara's deity (3) Third were the Aacharyas of Juna Akhara, followed by the Aacharya of Aawahan Akhara then the Shri Shri Maha-Mandaleshwaras of both the Akharas as per their seniority followed one another behind the Aacharyas (4) Fourth in sequence were the Naga saints of Juna and Aawahan, with their Palakies behind them.

Mass bathing at Kumbh

The number of Nagas who joined the Shahi was estimated to be about seven thousand. The carriages of the chief monks were pulled by householders and devotees. The seated ascetics were escorted by two bodyguards. *Chotiyas* carrying a *Chanwar* and a silver staff had covered the monks under a canopy. Anyone wearing leather shoes was not allowed to join the procession.

Pilgrims on both sides of the road crushed together to watch the grand show of Hindu monks. The crowd welcomed every passer by, each Mahatma being carried on a chariot. The devotees loudly cried *Har-Har Mahadev* and *Ganga Maiya ki Jai*, as they viewed them as perfect ascetics or Siddhas. The holy men would raise their hands in a mode of blessing. The Shahi procession reached its destination quickly. It had extended to a length of about two kilometres. Before crossing the bridge, the naked ascetics threw their garlands over the welcoming householders as a blessing. As soon as the procession moved onwards, the devotees, particularly the ladies, would rush to collect the sand bearing footprints of holy men. Others laid down on the ground saluting the image of footprints imprinted in the sand. Usually Indian *purdanasheen* ladies prefer to not see a naked man, yet at Kumbh, they view naked Sadhus and Sanyasi with the other Saints and Mahatmas as part of the religious Darshana ritual and believe that they will receive blessings for this act of devotion.

The main bathing ghat was totally vaccant for Juna Akhara. Other pilgrims had bathed in the margin time between two Akharas and had left the bathing ghat. A few naked holy men were displaying their physical powers. One Hatha Yogi joined the procession, hands raised up. His nerves were dried out and fingernails enlarged as a result of continuous practice for the

Mass bathing at Kumbh

Female monks after bathing at Kumbh

last several years. The procession of Shahi stopped on the sloped bed of the river confluence. Only the senior monks, particularly the saffron cloth wearers, moved to the river bed along with the deity—Akhara Dewata. Some naked holy men crouched here and there on the sandy bed and urinated. Others stood silently with their traditional weapons. The banners, Dhwaja, Danka and conveyances were at a distance of about 200 metres from the river. The Palki of Guru Maharaja stayed behind a few yards away from the Dewata at the river's

Mass bathing at Kumbh

confluence. The Naga group carrying the Akhara Deity worshipped on the riverbank. They entered the sacred water's depth along with the Dewata chanting loudly *Har-Har Mahadev*. After Akhara Dewata was given a holy dip in the confluence of the great rivers, naked holy men jumped into the sacred river from all sides.

Kumbh Mela and the Sadhus   76

First sacred bath of the Akhara deity

The Naga Sanyasi group headed by Sri Mahanta Santosh Giri came out of the river with the deity of the Akhara. They re-adorned and garlanded the deity with a sacred thread. The naked Nagas in their groups came out of the water and helped one another in smearing their bodies with ashes or sandy clay. A few naked holy men with open swords in their hands were shivering after a bath in the chilled water of the river. Now it was the turn of the senior monks who travelled on chariots to bathe in the river. They moved bare footed towards river's bed. The first group of householders accompanied their religious head, Shankaracharya.

He was escorted by two Naga bodyguards. One householder held a silver shoe in his hands, the *Khadau* of the holy priest. The Shankaracharya moved bare footed, wearing saffron clothes to his waist. The upper part

Female monks bathing at Kumbh

of his body was without any cloth. The religious heads in saffron clothes as Shankaracharya, Aacharya Maha Mandleshwara, Maha Mandeleshwara, Mandaleshwaras and the others did not bathe naked. They were accompanied under a saffron canopy up to the river's bed with their householder group of devotees. One part of the procession that had already bathed left the bathing ghat and was moving back toward

Crowd of pilgrims in mass bathing at Kumbh Prayag

Akhara. The female members, the *Nagin,* were the last to bathe in the river stream. They did not take off their clothes to avail a nude bath as they did at a previous Ardha Kumbh event. They took their bath at the sacred river's edge where it was difficult to even take a dip. Elderly female ascetics were shivering due to the cold. We availed a dip in a hurry.

The Shahi on its way back extended about 2 kilometres, up to the end of the next pontoon bridge. The naked ascetics carried the water of the sacred river in their personal *Kamandals.* Householders following the religious heads also carried metal pots full of water from the Sangam. The naked ascetics on their return journey were not as excited as they appeared at the starting point of the procession. The devotees standing on both sides of the return passage again ran eagerly to collect sand and clay bearing the footprints of the freshly washed monks.

The bathing ghat was approximately fifty metres wide. One could observe human heads in every direction from the Sangam. The capacity of the bathing platform was estimated to have been three hundred thousand persons per hour in 1989 whereas the actual inflow of the pilgrims in the bathing area at Sangam was about six hundred thousand persons per hour. In 1977, ten million people took the sacred bath here in a single day.

The Shahi entered into the Akhara at 9 a.m. The saints joined their fire pits to protect their bodies from the cold. The caretaker saints who stayed behind at the Akhara had made the food preparations now being served to the Shahi participants.

January 21st, 2001

The next sacred bathing occasion at Kumbh, was Mauni Amavasya, which attracts huge numbers of pilgrims and tourists. This particular day is important to Dasnaami Naga Sanyasi Akharas. They perform a number of rituals which start a day before Mauni Amavasya. Among the rituals were *Tanga-Toda Sanskara*, *Vyas Puja*,

Armed monk bathing

initiation of new Nagas and change of Akhara Sahibi. This day the Akhara Flag, Akhara Kalasha and the mobile deity *(Chala-Dewata)*, was encircled inside a boundary of ropes which restricted entry. Two Sanyasis holding silver rods and wearing saffron clothes guarded the location. The climate was nearly freezing.

On the way to Allahabad from Varanasi by road, the pilgrims were continuously moving with vehicles. Further on Jhunsi Road near Kumbh Nagar, the crowd appeared on foot. The crowd had a different shape this time. Early visitors to the Mela area had to find a place to stay till the bathing day. Among the visitors were children, ladies and heads of families. They moved ahead in a queue or sat on the roadside to rest. The crowd, made of mini groups of 5 - 10 persons, moved as a protective wall with members hand in hand or tied to one another, roped to a saree or dhoti. Each group pushed another to find its way. Penetrating by force, the crowd was entering Kumbh Nagar. The massive crush made people separate from their groups.

On both sides of the road there were a number of shops. Spreading various items on the sandy bed, the shops sold items like *Laichi Daana* (sugar balls), *Sindura* (vermilion) *Nariyala* (coconut), colourful threads, *Jadi-Buti* (herbs and medicines), bones of animals, incense, lockets, iron plates attached to a horse shoe *Nala*, *Shahi-Ka-*

Post bathing

Kata, *Kesher* (saffron), *Kasturi* (musk), *Munga* (coral), *Moti* (pearl), *Shankha* (conch) and religious books, etc. These shops were of a temporary nature settled at every two to five metres.

The pilgrims on foot visiting for one or two days would settle anywhere behind the temporary shops on the open land. I moved towards Daraganj following the chequered plate road from Jhunsi. Just beneath the Malviya Bridge on the western bank of the river Ganga, approximately five thousand readymade clay ovens were on sale along with cow dung for fuel. A few tea stalls, confectioners and shops selling milk packets were centralized in a mini-market. This locality was crowded with the pilgrims who had settled near their priest's house, a Dharamshala or with an acquaintance.

Tanga Toda Sanskara

Tanga Toda Sanskar at Kumbh

At about 6 a.m., the initiated newcomers, each with their Langoti Guru, visited the open land under the Akhara flag. The novitiate to be accepted into the Naga sect stands looking upward and salutes the Akhara flag. In the meantime, the Langoti Guru made his new disciples naked by opening the loincloth. Grabbing hold of the ascetic's penis, the teacher would then without any delay give it three jerks as a ritual of *Tanga-Toda Sanskara*. The ceremony as per the belief of the monks made the sex organ inactive for sexual pleasure. This particular ceremony was not open to the householders. As the Shahi was to proceed shortly, any entry of outsiders or householders was restricted at the Akhara entrance gate. Those who dared enter were taken out by force.

The sky was still dark due to fog. We came to know that a similar Tanga-Toda Sanskara of the female novitiates was being performed in a covered shade at Mai-Bara of Juna Akhara. The male members accepted into the Naga Sect and others first visited the Guru Maharaja at the Akhara flag to pay salutation in traditional naked manner. Sitting on the ground, knees folded, they kept their hands on the ground with fingers locked and looking upward. Then releasing the fingers, they prayed five times and recited *Om Guruji Namaha*. Upon completing the prayer, they bent their heads down to their hands, raising both thumbs up. On returning upright, they raised their heads with fully open eyes and chanted loudly *Om Namo Narayana*. The naked Nagas making a hand-to-hand grip with one another formed a queue for the Shahi. They were scrambling out of a chilling cold.

The saints whom Juna Akhara authorities had invited to join the Shahi now arrived with their householder devotees inside the Akhara campus. The householders held triangular mini flags of *Keshariya* colour.

Today the number of devotees following the saints was ten times more than the previous Shahi occasion. Other senior ascetics of Juna Akhara took an early morning bath inside the Akhara, smeared their bodies with ashes and sat around their Dhunis awaiting the Shahi to move out. Some moving yesterday in cloth were today naked. Those wearing a saffron cloth this time were among the Akhara Panch as elected representatives. They attached Akhara badges to their *Ganti* cloths and were authorised to implement the Akhara decisions at any moment. The Akhara people had banned the movement of any ascetic with his personal camera. The journalists were warned not to move with Shahi nor to make any sort of pictorial documentation.

Shahi Procession and Second Sacred Bath of the Akhara Deity

At about 6:45 a.m., ascetics from all the directions of their Madhi groups started coming out to visit Guru Maharaja beneath the Akhara flag. They paid respect to the deity then took to decorate themselves with garlands of marigold flowers. Their parade decoration hid their sex organs beneath the flowers. They joined a queue in four separate lines and carried their traditional weapons except a few who held guns as religious soldiers. The atmosphere was hazy when the Shahi was about to move at 7 a.m. The road in front of the Akhara gate was captured by the naked ascetics who pushed each other crying loudly 'Har-Har Mahadev'. The senior monks according to their Madhi groups were busy in commanding the uncontrolled religious madness, pushing and elbowing one another. The push and pull of the crowd attempting to stream out could be seen each time they allowed passage to a religious head who was entitled to ride on a Chariot (Palki).

Akhara Danka and Nisan came out at 7 a.m., followed by the Danka and Nisan of Aawahan Akhara to join the Shahi. Keeping a distance of

Chillum smoking at Kumbh

about 100 metres the Akhara Deity Dewta came out. The deity in a spear form, *Bhala,* was decorated with silver rings, garlands, flowers, saffron cloth and a lemon fixed to its upper tip. Within a short moment the Deity of Aawahan Akhara joined adjacent to Juna.

This time the Shahi had two Palkis, one the Deity Dutta Maharaja and another Ista Gajnana from Juna and Aawahan respectively. The rest of the queue sequence order followed arrangements as usual. This day's Shahi was considerably longer, ten times greater than the Shahi of January 14th.

It took more than 15 minutes for the procession end to move out from its originating point. The procession was expected to extend three kilometres in length, the human line with naked ascetics estimated to be approximately thirty thousand in number. A total of 22 tractors were included as decorated chariot seats to carry the religious heads. The tractors at the end carried the old female Nagins of the sect.

The Akhara Deity was carried to the riverbank and ceremonial worship continued for five minutes. At the end of the rituals they entered into the river's streams, moving ahead about ten metres distance along with the Deity. The front of the Deity was dipped into the river Ganga. The naked Nagas as per their routine urinated on the bathing ghats and jumped into the river stream as they saw the Deity bathing in the river. The naked ascetics took twenty minutes to bathe in the holy river's stream at the confluence then moved back on their way to the Akhara via another route. The Shahi moved 0.5 kilometre on its way back when the religious heads came down from their seats in the Palki and Rathas. Most of them wore a saffron *Dhoti* tied at their waist. They moved bare footed to the river. A householder, following the religious head Shankaracharya, held a silver *Khadau* in his hands and carried it to the river's bank. Three hundred or more lady monks were last in line to dip.

They changed their wet clothes at the water's edge and returned back to the Akhara procession. A few senior monks, still busy in administration of the procession on the ghats, were the very last to avail a holy dip. Sri Mahanta Prem Giri, Mahanta Hari Giri and others wore saffron clothes. Sri Mahanta Prem Giri availed his holy immersion naked.

The timing of Shahi procession: 7 a.m.; Sangam arrival: 8 a.m.; Sangam bathing: 40 minutes; Sangam departure: 8:40 a.m.; Akhara return: 9 a.m. The senior monks and the religious heads on Chariots that assembled at the Shahi of Juna Akhara, on their return to Akhara, attended the high platform beneath the Akhara flag. They made cash donations to the Akhara called the Danka-Dana. On receiving the cash donation the Sri Mahantas Secretaries cried out loudly '*Sri Panch Das Naam Guru Murtiyo Sunana Ji , Sri...* (Name of donor and title) *ne Sri Guru Maharaja Ki Sewa Puja me Rupaya ...* (amount) *Bhet me Diya'*. At the end of each announcement, one Naga at a corner beat two drums.

Immediately on end of the bathing procession, the attendants of Shahi were offered breakfast at every Dhuni. Madhi group Marshals were busy accompanying the newly initiated Nagas, introducing them into the Akhara

Devotees at Kum

community.The rest of the Akharas moved according to a mutual settlement by seven Sanyasi Akharas atAllahabad on 9th February 1989.

Basant Panchami Day, Kumbh Prayag

The third and last Shahi procession of the Naga ascetics is taken on Basant Panchami day, when the deity of the Akhara receives its third sacred bath in the holy river and the ascetics take a royal bath as previously.

The *Nayi Sarkaar* or *Sahibi* changes at each successive Kumbh and Ardha Kumbh fair at Prayag. The Juna Akhara elects a new executive body, *Sahibi*, who will admnistrate for six years, on Basant Panchami day. The Shambhu Panch elects the new members of the Ramata Panch. The Presidential power is also rotated to another Madhi group.

The Naga sect follows more rituals prior to the departure of Akhara from Kumbh Nagar after Basant Panchami. The general assembly of the Naga sect, the invitees and the religious heads join a mass meal called *Pangata*. They are served food prepared with gram flour boiled with spices and curd along with another dish of pudding fried in oil called *Kadhi* and *Pakauda*. The ritual on the name of the food served is called *Kadhi-Pakaude Ki Rasma*. It is a kind of thanksgiving ceremony for those who made the Shahi a grand success.

The Mela area allotted to Juna Akhara dismantles after the departure of *Chala-Devata*,the mobile Deity, in the form of *Varuna-Kalasha*, which settled beneath the Akhara Flag on the day of *Dhwaja Rohana* and *Bhumi Pujana*.

Since the Deity is invited by the Akhara, it is asked to depart on completion of the Kumbh ritual called *Visarjan* of *Varun Kalash*. The Dewata Panch now carries the Akhara Deity *Bhala* to Akhara head office premises in Varanasi. It involves a five day journey on foot by a group of ascetics after which the Akhara flag comes down from its base.

Indian householder ladies showing their regard/gratitude to a holy man at Juna Akhara

Attending Danka-Daan Calls

Vaishnava Sadhus preparing food

Order of Shahi for the Das Naam Akharas at Kumbh and Ardha-Kumbh

The Akharas to move under their order of preference

At Kumbh *Prayag* on the three bathing days, Maha Nirvani Akhara is to avail first bath.
Niranjani Akhara accompanied by Nirvani, Atal and Ananda Akhara to avail a bath after Maha Nirvani Akhara Juna.
Aawahana Akharas combined together with Agni Akhara to follow behind Niranjani Akharas as third in order.

Kumbh *Haridwar,* there are three bathing days. On Shiva Ratri, Sri Juna Bhairo Akhara to avail first.
On Amavasya, Sri Niranjani Akhara is to avail first bath and Sri Panch Das Naam Juna Akhara to follow behind Sankranti Niranjani Akhara at a distance of 50 yards.

At Kumbh *Ujjain,* the Order of Shahi shall be with the sign of Dutta Bhagwana in front, Akhara 'Nishan'. 'Sawari' of Peerji on the elephant and the followers behind Peerji. Then Juna, Maha Nirvani and Niranjani Akharas to accompany and move as parallel and equally.

At Kumbh *Nasik,* on the way to Kushawarta bank, Nirwani and Atal Akharas are to move parallel and equally with the 'Palqui' at the back.

Forehead markings of the holymen and devotees

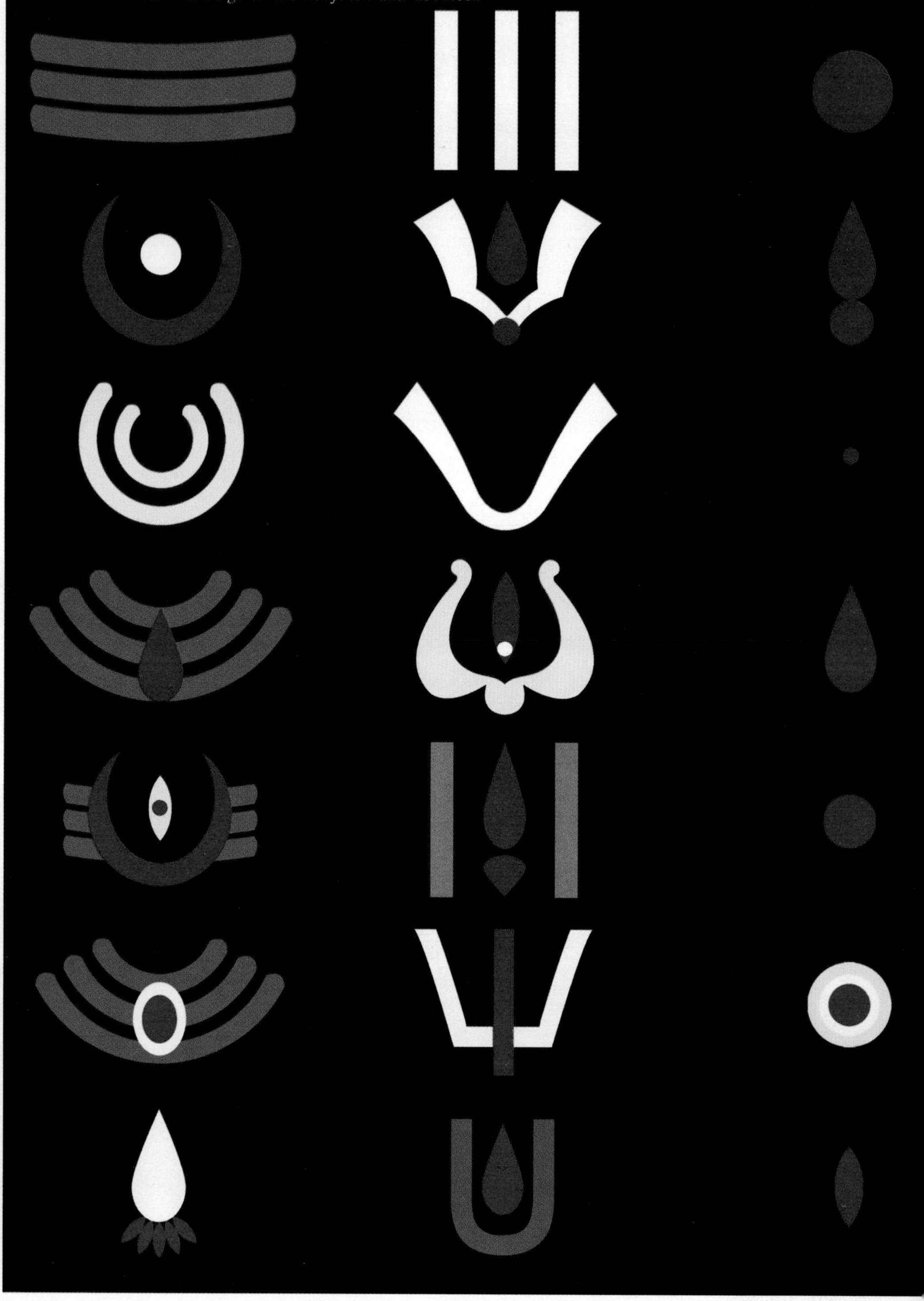

Chapter 5
Post Kumbh Rituals in Varanasi

Traditionally, the Kumbh Prayag begins in the inner sanctum of the river Ganga at Allahabad and it ends in Varanasi, also on the bank of the sacred river Ganga. Even for householders, the Kumbh and Ardha Kumbh Prayag finishes after a holy bath at Varanasi. Two more Kumbh bathing events were to be held in Allahabad on coming days with participation of the other worshippers. However, within ten days the Naga sadhus had completed three great Shahi bathing ceremonies and other rituals and were ready to travel on.

During the Kumbh 2001, the Panch and Akhara saints returned to the ancient, revered city of Varanasi from the Prayag Kumbh Mela on the very next day as per the available mode of conveyance after Basant Panchami festival. The Ramata Panch who carry the movable properties and Akhara Dewata, had to complete a distance of 120 kilometres from Kumbh Nagar to Varanasi in a period of five days. During this time the senior Buddha Panch members settle at Akhara headquarters and branch offices to look after the affairs.

Naga Sadhus at Varanasi on Shivaratri Day
Every six years, the event of Shiva Ratri in Varanasi becomes the fourth sacred bathing occasion of Kumbh and Ardha Kumbh at Allahabad.

The Naga Sanyasi Akhara has a tradition of moving out from

Kumbh Mela and the Sadhus

Kumbh Allahabad after having availed the sacred bath and Shahi three times. On Shiva-Ratri they join other religious parades to visit the supreme Lord Shiva temples in Nepal at Pashupati Nath temple and in India at Junagarh and Kashi Viswanatha temples.

The Naga ascetics make claims of their participation in the religious battles against the Muslim rulers and icon breaker invaders in the holy city of Varanasi when the temple structure existed at the site of the present Gyanwapi Mosque.

Nagas worshiping the Shiva Lingam at Kashi Vishwanatha

Their participation in fights to protect that ancient temple earned them the right they avail presently to worship the Lingam of the deity Kashi Vishwanatha at Varanasi in top order of priority. At Varanasi they form a religious procession and move out naked for worship of the patron deity of the city, Lord Shiva in Lingam form, at Kashi Vishwanatha temple.

Naga Procession and Worship

The Nagas, holy men and holy women returning from Kumbh Prayag stay in Varanasi, in and near Juna Akhara surroundings, for a period of about sixty days. The Naga holy men of other Shiva Akharas also join their offices at Varanasi during this period. Juna Akhara invites all seven

Shaiva Akharas to join the procession and worship at Kashi Viswanatha temple but the Shiva Ratri procession does not involve any sacred bathing of the Nagas with the Akhara Deity in the river at Varanasi.

The Akhara Danka, Nisana, Dhwaja, Dewata and Charana Paduka are taken out to lead the procession followed by the naked ascetics with Palki and Sawari of the religious heads on the Shiva Ratri Day, which is the last specific Kumbh occasion. They march from Hanumana Ghat to the Chowk locality following the city road route via Madanpura and Godaulia. The naked holy men move out ash-smeared, bare footed, either displaying their physical arts or in a queue. The female monks followed the procession last. Reaching Gyanwapi road, the entrance passage towards Kashi Viswanatha turns down about two metres through the steps and follows a narrow lane.

Sadhus at Annapurna Temple

The Akhara Flag, Danka, Elephant and Palanquin turned back after reaching this point. The holy men reassembled after worship of the deities Lord Shiva, Annapurna and Dhundhiraja Ganesha. Just to the side of Gyanwapi Mosque, the holy men reached an open platform near the Gyanwapi well. The time allotted to the holy men was 40 minutes in the early morning at 7 a.m.

During their worship period, the entry of ordinary people inside the temple was restricted. The crowd of devotees waited for the temple enclosures to be opened and during that time they watched the naked holy men with curiosity. The Kashi Viswanatha Temple administration provided one Maund (approximately 40 litres) of milk and Ganga water inside the temple enclosures to facilitate the holy men in completing their worship. They took Kamandals full of Ganga water with milk to offer prayers in the inner sanctum of the supreme Lord Shiva .

The deity in a lingam form is a self-born deity, worshiped as *Jyotira Lingam*. The holy men offered flowers, *Bel-patra* (Bilva leaves), *Madara* fruit and sacred water (Ganga Jal) of the river Ganga which they poured over the lingam. The temple priest inside the inner sanctum helped them to worship the deity. The main religious teachers, the Aacharya Mahamandaleshwara and others were asked to make donations to the priest performing the rituals. A video camera fixed to the top corner inside the inner sanctum captured the events.

Next to Vishwanatha they visited the Goddess Annapurna temple at a short distance. The procession returned back through the side of Dhundhi Raja Lane towards Bansphatak Road and ended inside the Akhara, where the main religious heads assembled together.

After the Shiva Ratri procession the 'field formation' unit of the Akhara, called Ramata Panch, is separated from the static formation—the Buddha Panch and the Akhara head office. The Ramata Panch moves out to wander on foot until reaching the next Kumbh location.

The Tradition of Samadhi

Samadhi is a state of suspended bodily animation while the conscious awareness departs in deep meditation or at death. Some saints such as Sri Ramakrishna have demonstrated spontaneous samadhi for days at a time, when he appeared lifeless but was actually in profound meditation.

A monument constructed over the remains of a deceased saint is also called a Samadhi. One can visit the humble or elaborate Samadhis of many departed saints, such as Sri Aurobindo or Mata Amritanandamayima. Samadhi also denotes a Yogic posture known as Padmasana, i.e., framing the body in a sitting posture like a reverse triangle. Usually Samadhi means to bury the saints physical body underground or underwater in the Padmasana sitting posture.

To place one's

Return Journey (Olaf Rocksien)

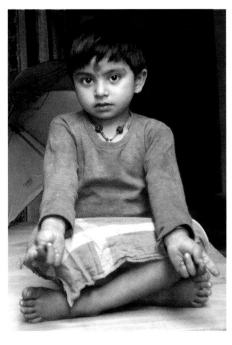

living body in Samadhi for a period of sixty to seventy hours or more as a part of miraculous show can be observed during Kumbh. The monks prepare their body through Yogic practices before they undergo a state of Samadhi in public. To place one's body covered underground in a sitting posture of Samadhi requires control over one's breathing cycles to regulate a limited supply of oxygen. In order to overcome the supply of oxygen during the specified period, an area near a water source is generally selected and carbon dioxide released by the body is removed through the outlets which are covered tactfully by garlands, flowers and sand, etc. The platform so erected becomes a place of worship and a religious spot for devotees who offer monetary donations.

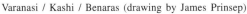
Varanasi / Kashi / Benaras (drawing by James Prinsep)

The soul having left the body of a holy man, the Sanyasi or Sadhu is immediately framed into the posture of Samadhi or the ascetic himself may enjoin the triangular posture of Samadhi by himself before consciously attaining death. The dead body of a Hindu holy man is never burnt as Hindus usually do, rather it is buried in a posture of Samadhi underground and a monument erected or is dropped into the running water of a river.

Kumbh at Varanasi

After death, the posture of the body should always be sitting, whereas the dead body of a householder is laid down in sleeping posture on a pyre to follow the funeral fire rites.

As a general rule the holy man has renounced all the worldly possessions except his own body and he would not will for death. The Hindu monks meditate in peace for a long time in the Padmasana posture of Samadhi and they may avail a willing death in Samadhi following certain Yogic activities. If they prefer to not delay their death they would attempt a wished death . The saints would recall 'O death, thou acting to cause delay in my death, I myself, availing the Yogic activities, leave this physical body'. The name of a dead monk is followed by the word *Brahmaleena* (gone to Brahma), meaning one merged into the god. The place of Samadhi, if marked by a monument, becomes a place of Worship for the Hindus. The right of performing the death rites to the dead body in Samadhi goes to the disciple who acts as a successor either by merit of seniority or decided by the senior members of the Akhara.

To the left side of the entrance gate of the Akhara, one old Sanyasi of 04 Madhi expired at midnight. His body was settled by two disciples into a posture of Samadhi, cross-legged and ornamented with garlands of marigold flowers. The Akhara authorities (senior monks) were busy in making arrangements for the *Jal Samadhi* of the body of the dead ascetic. The ritual was to be performed in the river streams at Sangam where the pilgrims took a sacred bath.

After Death Ceremony

The disciples of the deceased Naga saint as a pre-funeral rite of Samadhi, placed on the shoulders of the dead body a bag *(Jholi)* which contained in it one large bread called *Rota* as a meal and one *Chilama* (clay-pipe) filled with *Ganja* (cannabis). The Rota was made of whole-wheat flour about twelve inches in diameter and one inch thick. The dead body was then shifted inside the four-wheeler. An emergency pantoon bridge number zero was opened for them to carry their member in Samadhi. One sector magistrate garlanded the dead ascetic and went with the vehicle.

As a ritual of *Jal-Samadhi* (Water-Samadhi) to the dead Naga Sanyasi, they dropped the body at a distance of about twenty metres from the bathing area mid-way in the river. After performing the Samadhi ritual they went just behind the bathing area where the monks aboard the boat took a sacred bath at Sangam.

The Naga saints accompanying the group bathed at this location naked, washed their clothes and redressed themselves in saffron clothes.

The Holy Bath at Kumbh

Kumbh fair attracts the largest crowd of salvation seekers on earth. The great bath is held on Parva days when the the elixir of immortality is available. The bathing ghat at Prayag Sangam provides the householder a platform to seek salvation through deeds, devotion, knowledge and renunciation, i.e., "*Karma, Bhakti, Gyana and Vairagya.*"

Kumbh provides the essentials of mental peace to all living creatures and reveals the theory of immortality of the soul.

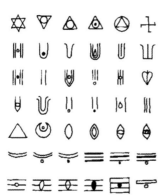

Tikka (Olaf Rocksien)

Horizontal row 1 from left to right: items 1-5 Brahma and/or theTrimurti.

Horizontal rows 2-4: Visnu and his followers - Vaisnavas or Vaishnavites

Horizontal rows 5-7: Siva and/of his followers - Saivas or Shaivites.

AKHARAS AT KUMBH

The Sadhus are seen in four major categories:

Nagas (Sanyasi), Vairagi (Mundies), Udasi, and Nirmala (Nanak Shahi). They are organized into different Akharas and join Shahi to avail mass bathing in this order:

- **The Shaivite Sadhus titled Naga (Sanyasi):**
  those who express their faith in Lord Shiva.
  1. Shri Taponidhi Niranjani Akhara Panchayati
  2. Shri Panchayati Anand Akhara
  3. Shri Panchadashnam Juna Akhara
  4. Shri Panch Ahvahan Akhara
  5. Shri Agni Akhara
  6. Shri Panchayati Akhara Maha Nirvani
  7. Shri Panch Atal Akhara

- **The Vaishnava Sadhus titled Vairagi (Mundies):**
  those who express their faith in Lord Vishnu.
  8. Nirmohi
  9. Digamber
  10. Nirwani

- **The Vaishnava Sadhus titled Udasi:**
  11. Naya Panchayati Udasin Akhara
  12. Bada Panchayati Udasin Akhara

- **The Vaishnava Sadhus titled Nirmala or Nanak Panthi:**
  13. Nirmala Akhara

Churning of the Ocean

The churning of the primeval ocean symbolises the creation of the ordered universe out of chaos. It is a story about the eternal struggle between the two cosmic opposites good (*dharma*) and evil (*adharma*)

Mohini serving Amrit to the Devas and Asuras

between gods - *devas* - and demons – *asuras,* light versus darkness.

It was nearly the end of that dark age called *Kaliyuga,* demons ruled the universe, and men failed in piety. The Amrita had been lost during one of the periodical cosmic deluges, and this loss had weakened the gods as well as the men.

The gods met on Mount Meru and decided to ask *Brahma,* the Lord of Creation, for help. Lord Brahma said: Our vital Amrita and Soma lies hidden in the ocean. Just as golden butter is churned out from silver white milk, so we need to separate the divine liqueur from the seawater. Go worship Lord Visnu. He will help you.

The gods gladly sang Visnusahasranama, the thousand names of Lord Visnu. Lord Visnu determined that Amrita would revive the gods and that to find it, all the gods and demons together would have to churn the ocean.

He reassured the gods to maintain their faith in Him.

The king of serpents, *Vasuki,* coiled himself around Mount Mandara like a spiraled rope and the gods and demons alternately pulled at his head and tail to spin the mountain like a churning rod.

After one thousand years of churning, Mount Mandara was slipping into the deep mud of the wildly swirling sea. Lord Visnu then incarnated as Kurma, a tortoise as big as a continent. Kurma slipped deep underneath the ocean to support Mount Mandara.

As the churning continued, fourteen precious things were revealed or found: the Sun - *Surya* - the Moon - *Soma* - and the Stars, the ruby adornment for *Visnu's* chest, the coral Tree of Life, the Conch and the Bow, the wish-yielding cow, the sacred cow, the white elephant mount of *Indra*, and the moonlight mare mount of the demon king *Bali*. The *Apsaras,* bewitching celestial nymphs, emerged as did *Varuni,* the goddess of wisdom and *Laksmi,* the goddess of wealth and fertility. Laksmi held a lotus and Lord Visnu, the father of the three worlds, recognized her as his *Sakti*.

Finally appeared *Dhanvantari,* author of the *AyurVeda,* doctor to the gods and another manifestation of Lord Visnu, holding a bowl full of divine *amrta*. A soon as he emerged, the gods and demons dropped the serpent churning rope and madly ran toward toward *Dhanvantari* to grab the bowl. The demons seized the *Amrita*, then fought amongst each

Painting by B.D Pandey

other for who would drink first. In the midst this dispute, *Mohini,* a celestial seductress beyond the power of words, appeared. The demons were distracted by *Mohini'*s dazzling beauty. One of the demons gripping the bowl suggested that she should decide how the divine drink of life should be shared. *Mohini* smiled and the demons all agreed to trust her choice. *Mohini* said that both gods and demons had worked equally hard to obtain the *Amrita.* so it should be shared equally. She had them all form two rows and close their eyes. As an incarnation of Maya, Lord Visnu's power of delusion, Mohini took the bowl and served the row of gods first. After all of the gods had been served by this seductress, she disappearred

The gods had regained strength from the Amrita and easily won the ensuing battle which restored the righteous balance of the universe. Disguising himself as a god, the demon *Rahu* had stealthily entered into the row of gods and received a drop of *amrita* before he was recognized. Lord Vishnu immediately threw his solar disc, the *Sudarsana Cakra,* which decapitated the demon before the taste of *Amrita* could reach his body. Rahu's body fell dead but the disc flung his now immortal head into space. Rahu lives as a revengeful planet between the Sun and Moon. Eclipses are caused by his trying to devour them. Planets possess consciousness and have the power to influence and to act. They have presiding gods whom they obey.

Text adapted from a version by Paul de Smedt

Samudra Manthan (Painting B.D. Pandey)

Kumbh and World Peace

One of the world conquerors, Alexander the Great, was on his way to subdue the next country. While passing through the dense forests and across the deep rivers of the Indian subcontinent, he saw a sadhu peacefully relaxing under a tree next to his little tent camp. The conqueror decided to sit close to him for a little rest of his own.

The sadhu asked Alexander, "Who are you? Where are you going and what is your dream?"

The conqueror answered that he was on his way to make war on the neighboring country to attain victory.

The Sadhu then asked, "What will you do after winning that country?" Alexander answered, "I shall plan to win the next country."

The Saint asked Alexander again, "and then what?" to which the conqueror replied, "I shall conquer the next one."

The Sadhu smiled and said, "Suppose you conquer the entire world, then what will you do?" Alexander's answered. "Then I shall relax in peace."

The Sadhu burst into laughter and suggested, "You'd better relax and be in peace here."

This story is often shared by the great saints, fakirs, priests and thinkers such as the Shankarcharyas and His Holiness Dalai Lama.

Pilgrims at Kumbh

Chapter 6

Glorious Glimpses of Haridwar and Kumbh Mela 2010

Kumbh Parva at Haridwar

The essential feature for the occurrence of the Kumbh Parva at Haridwar is a combination of heavenly bodies, the Sun in Aries and Jupiter in Aquarius and the Moon in Cancer

Padmininayako Meshe Kumbhrashau Yada Guruh
Gangadwar Bhawadayogah Kumbhnama Tadottamah

The importance of Haridwar Tirtha and the Kumbh Parva being organised here at regular intervals is well known. The holy cities bestowing salvation to the Hindus in the Indian sub continent are Ayodhya, Mathura, Kashi, Maya-Haridwar, Awantika-Ujjain, Kanchi, and Dwarika. No other city can be compared with these salvation bestowing cities.

The religious verses in praise of the Kumbh Parva at Haridwar "Saa Vidyaparmamukter- Hetubhoota Sanatani" says that the supernatural power, Goddess Maya, established that this very location had once handled the Kumbh-Pot combining the elixir of immortality—the Amrit. It is said that bathing in Kankhal Tirth during a full Kumbh at Haridwar entitles the devotees to avail the benefits of the supreme goals.

The fruits of a holy dip in the Ganga at Haridwar find no comparison in the reward of righteous deeds the spiritual acts of a thousand Ashwamedhas and hundreds of Vedic sacrifices. In fact the Kumbh at Haridwar helps mankind to avail the goals of life as Dharma, Artha, Kaam, and Moksha.

Sadhus entering in the Kumbh

Kumbh Parva, Where and What

Some scholars are of the opinion that the Kumbh occurs with a combination of planets (the Sun, the Moon and Jupiter). Jupiter gains more importance for the reason that it is the teacher of the Gods and protected the nectar pot from the demons. Considering the fact that Jupiter does not combine Aquarius (Kumbh) on the other three Kumbh spots, the tradition of Kumbh originated in Haridwar. The position of Jupiter in different zodiac signs (Aries, Leo, Taurus and Aquarius) which adds importance to the Kumbh Parva at four different locations

The Mysterious energy of Kumbh Parva

Kumbh brings mysterious energy to the river bank when the planetary orbit cycle coincides with a precise combination of the stars. Water, which is most easily influenced by any energy, is considered to attract and absorb the cosmic energy generated in the universe at different combinations of the planetary orbits, especially when Kumbh Parva occurs at Haridwar, Ujjain, Nasik and Allahabad.

The modern scientists accept that cosmic energy reaching the earth combine with the sources of river water in an area of 45 kilometres to give medicinal qualities and other cosmic electrical magnetic effects which are beneficial to a devotee bathing at that moment on the river bank. It is also believed that the sacred water collected from the Kumbh during the Parva days, if stored in a non conductive pot, e.g., lead, plastic or wood, preserve the mysterious energy for a long time. The devotees for this very reason carry home the water of the sacred river in cans or sealed jars after a holy dip during Kumbh.

There are two significant spots in Haridwar, the first is near Neel Dhara, another is Brahma Kunda at Har ki Pauri bestowing mysterious energy helpful to the living creatures during Kumbh.

श्री मणि रंभा वारुणी अमिय शंख गजराज, कल्पद्रुम धनु धेनु शशि धन्वन्तरि विष बाज।

Haridwar Tirtha

Haridwar is considered as a Tirtha and a holy city by the Hindus and also one of the salvation bestowing puries amongst the seven holy cities. It is located in between the Shivalik range of the Himalayas and on the right bank of river Ganga there is a chain of Neel Parvat in the east and Bilva Parvat in the west at a height of about 1000 feet above sea level in Uttarakhand state.

Nagas at Ghat for Shahi Snan

Haridwar has several names, such as *Mayapur, Hardwar, Haridwar, Gangdwara, Mayurpur, Kapilsthan, and Papawan* etc. But, it is still difficult to determine the exact time of naming the city Haridwar. This location is identified in the ancient religious books as *Maya Kshetra* Haridwar and extended upto Rishikesh. Still, there is a difference of opinion upon the names *'Hardwar'* and *'Haridwar'*. The *Shaivist* call it *Hardwar* and the *Vaishnawas* recognise it as *Haridwar*. The followers of both the *Shaivist* and *Vaishnavas* express equal affection and faith to this holy city.

The holiest of holy rivers Ganga emerging from Gangotri in the Himalaya is first visible in the plains only at Haridwar. Before this point the river flows in between the dense forest sloping downwards. Hence, this location where the river meets the plains is known as *Gangdwar* in the religious texts and *Puranas. Gangdwar* means the gateway to the river Ganga. While examining the *Purans,* we find the seven *'Puries'* in two equal halves of three and a half *Puries*— *Vishnu Puries* and the other being *Shiv Puries.* Since the old name *Mayapur* disappeared, the city is called *Hardwar* representing *Shiva Puri* or a city devoted to Lord Shiva.

The city leads towards *Badri Naraian* and *Kailash Maansarovar*. Since, *Badri Narain* is devoted to a Hindu deity (Lord *Vishnu*) of the *Vaishnawas,* they call this emerging point leading upward as *Haridwar*. Whereas, the *Shaivist* call it *Hardwar,* a gate way to Lord *Shiva* as the land connects the pilgrims to *Kailash Maansarovar.* The different names of the city mean "gateway to heaven", "gateway to Lord Shiva", "gateway to Lord Vishnu". The scene of this holy city is very charming and attractive as the river touches its bank with clean river water and in full flow. The Rigveda recognises the river Ganga as the first river amongst all the holy rivers. *Skand Puran* states, *"Na Tirtham Gangya Samam"* there is no *Tirtha* equivalent to the river Ganga. *Jagat Guru Aadi Shankaracharya* also praised the river in *Ganga Stawan :*

> *Dev Sureshwari Bhagwati Gange,*
> *Tribhuwan Tarini Taral Tarange*
> *Shanker Mauli Viharini Vimale,*
> *Mam Matirastam Tav Pad Kamle*

Padam Puran in praise of Haridwar says *"Haridwarasya Sadrusham Shakraprasthgatasya Wai, Na Tirtham Loke Chaturvarga Falpradam"* this *Tirtha* bestows *Dharma, Artha, Kaam, Moksha* — the four basic aims of the humans on this earth. It may be enchanted that no other Tirtha is capable of providing the four basic pursuits of life, other than Haridwar.

Brahmakund or Hari ki Pairi

Brahmakunda is associated with a mythological story of penance by King *Shweta* to please Lord *Brahma,* when King *Bhagiratha* brought the river Ganga from heaven to this earth. Lord *Brahma,* being pleased with the penance, blessed him and confirmed his stay with Lord *Vishnu* and Lord *Shiva* at the spot of penance. Lord *Brahma* also blessed the King that the land will be known in the name of Lord Brahma and the entire Tirtha would reside at this very junction. This location is known as *Brahmakunda* since then. King *Vikramaditya* enriched the bank of the river fronting the city with permanent steps, since then the location is famous as *'Hari ki Pairi'.*

Temple of Shrawan Nathji

The temple of Shrawan Nath ji is situated to the south of Kushawarta Tirtha. Swrawan Nath ji was a Mahatma, a perfect saint in the true sense and known for his miraculous powers. He converted the water of the river Ganga into *Ghee,* during the mass assembly of the Sadhus at the 1901 Kumbh. He was also cross examined by a yogini, who presented before Baba Shrawan Nath one pot and asked him to fill it with a sweet pudding - *Kheer.* The mythological story of the miraculous powers of the yogini and Baba Shrawan Nath as the pot continued to be filled with *Kheer* for hours and the *Kamandal* of *Babaji* containing it could not be emptied. The temple houses an image of a five faced diety Mahadev.

Kushawart

To the south of *Brahmakunda,* at a short distance there is *Mahatirtha Kushawart.* People visit this place to offer an after death rite of their deceased ancestors and perform *Pinda Daan.* It is assumed that a holy bath at this place bestows salvation, and he gets rid of the cycle of births and rebirths. This place attracts a great crowd on *Mesha Sankranti.* The *Skand Puran* gives in praise to this Tirtha. To the west from Haridwar, is a mountain called *Bilwa,* where a Shiva temple is situated. The temple is famous as *Bilwakeshwara.* As per the mythological stories, the Goddess Sati entered into a great penance at this place consuming the leaves of the *Bilva* tree to please Lord Shiva as he would be her husband.

Chiefs of various disciplines deciding the Shahi Snan plans in their apex body Akhara Parishad.

Kumbh Administrator Anand Bardhan and DIG of Kumbh Alok Sharma welcoming traditional Shahi Peshwai of the Akharas.

Neel Dhara

The stream of the holy river Ganga flowing below *Neel Parvata* mountain is called *Neel Dhara*. A sacred bath at *Neel Dhara* followed by the worship of *Neeleshwar Mahadev* is considered to be of great significance. It is said that one of the disciple - *Gana* of Lord Shiva named *Neel* entered into great penance to please Lord Shiva, since then the mountain is called *Neel Parvat* and *Shiva Linga* established by him is called *Neeleshwara*.

Kankhal

> *Khala Ko Naatra Muktim wai Bhajate Tatra Majjanat*
> *Atah Kankhalam Tirtham Namna Chakramunishwarah*

Meaning, there is no *Khal* (the evil) who would not avail salvation after a holy bath here. It is located to the south of Haridwar and here the houses *(Mathas and Akharas)* of *sanyasis* and *sadhus* are in great numbers.

Sri Maya Devi *(The supreme female power of Haridwar)*

The presiding deity of *Mayapuri* (Hardwar) is *Dewa 'Daksheshwar Mahadeva'* and the presiding female deity is *Devi Bhagawati 'Maya Devi'*. On the authority of the chapter of *Kedar Khand* under *Skand Puran,* it is proved that *Dakshiyani Sati* and the presiding female deity of *Mayapuri* are the same. Goddess *Mayadevi* of Haridwar is the daughter of King *Daksha,* who was first *Manas Putra* of Lord Brahma ji, Goddess Mayadevi who was later married to Lord Shiva, was also known as *Sati.* The temple of the goddess is to the north of a sacrifice tower where *Daksha Prajapati* the father of Goddess *Sati* once invited Gods for *Yagya* - a great religious gathering. As per the mythological stories Goddess *Sati* visited this very place of her father on the eve of the great sacrifice *(Yagya)*, in absence of invitation from her father, she did not find the share of sacrifice for Lord Shiva. Being unhappy and annoyed with this insult to her husband, she separated her body from her soul by her yogic powers. This caused Lord Shiva to become enraged and he completely destroyed the sacrificial ceremony and separated the head of King Daksha from his body. After a petition of mercy by the Gods, Lord Shiva made King Daksha alive by attaching the head of a goat to his body. Lord Shiva blessed the land to be famous in the name of Goddess *Sati.* Lord Shiva is seen here in the form of *Aanand Bhairo.* To the north of Maya Devi temple, a place associated with Sri Panch Dasnaam Juna Akhara. The temple was destroyed by Taimur Lang in 1398.

First Kumbh of Uttarakhand State

The newly formed Uttarakhand state hosted its first Kumbh Mela at Haridwar, headed by the Honorable Chief Minister of the State Dr. Ramesh Pokhariyal 'Nishank'. This Mela has become known for a number of events adopted for the first time. Kumbh 2010 witnessed the arrival of huge numbers of pilgrims in densely packed trains, buses, tractors, bullock carts and with pets. Many of them reached by walk, carrying the their luggage on their heads. Some very rich and prosperous people availed aeroplanes and helicopters to come to the Kumbh. One of the private companies Prabhatam introduced for the first time helicopter services at cheap rates for the pilgrims. Upto January 2010 each and every hotel, Dharmashala and personal residences were filled with devotees, those who could not get shelter, halted at railway stations and at the bathing ghats.

The Mela area was divided into eleven sectors upto Kankhal and Rishikesh covering an area of 99,65,600 square feet. The major ten Akharas; Niranjani, Juna, Maha Nirwani, Awahan, Agni, Aanad, Atal, Nirmal, Panchayati Akhara Bada Udaseen, Naya Udaseen Akhara were settled in Mahamandleshwar Nagar, Gaurishankar and Dakshadweep sectors, the Vairagi Akharas in the Sati Dweep and Daksha Dweep Sectors in an area of 64 hundred thousand square feet of land.

The religious heads of the Akharas and other social non profit making organisations participated in Kumbh 2010, where the religious heads of the Akharas marked their Mela entry with pomp and show. Chief Ministers of other states and Members of Parliament participated in workshops on the river Ganga prior to the environment of the Kumbh and visited the main bathing days.

According to Mr. Pankaj Sehgal, a prominent businessman, it was for the first time that the devotees and customers were allowed to stay in the local markets to fulfil their needs. The facility of direct approach of the tourist inside the market made even the smallest businessman happy during this Kumbh.

High-tech Kumbh

This Kumbh was completely high-tech in which the technology was used to guide pilgrims and provide safety with facilities. The entire Kumbh area was under surveillance through 22 closed circuit cameras and LCD television screens displaying the actual position of the crowd on the ghats. About 1500 loudspeakers were installed to identify lost and found persons in the crowd.

Rare Astronomical Combinations and Traditions

The Kumbh 2010 at Haridwar witnessed a number of rare astronomical combinations. The second bathing day to occur on the 15th of January witnessed a solar eclipse after a period of 1330 years. During the occasion of *Basant Panchami* and *Maha Shivaratri* made a rare combination of Stars after 331 years. The Last Shahi bath on the14th April witnessed a religious combination of stars after 3333 years.

For the first time in the history of Kumbh Mela. The Akhara Parishad approved four Shahi snan in place of the traditional three Shahi snan. The mass bathing on Chaitra Purnima was recognised as a Shahi Snan at this Kumbh.

It was also a historical decision that Three Bairagi Akharas, two Udasin Akharas with Nirmal Akhara joined the first Shahi Snan on Maha Shivaratri day with other Shavatic Akharas. It was the first time after 250 years.

A new tradition was established by the Chief Minister of Uttarankhand State, Dr. Ramesh Pokhariyal alongwith his wife, as a common devotee took a late mid-night bath (on January 14th and 15th) in the holy river Ganga at Hari Ki Pairi without any administrative officials and security. He examined the security arrangements as well as the facilities provided by the administration. He also cross examined the situation from the pilgrims bathing at that moment. Not only the common men but also the Sadhus and Sanyasis were guided on very complex matters by the President of the Akhara Parishad, Acharya Vishwadewanand, Mahant Mitra Prakash, Mahant Rajendra Das, and Mahant Mahendra Singh Nirmal etc.

The Religious head of Atal Akhara Acharya Maha Mandaleshwara Mahant Sukhdewanand involved himself in teaching the devotees in his Pandal regarding the secrets of the Tantra and Mantra worship method and subjects like pity to the birds and animals. Sri Sriyantra Temple being prepared by the Nirwani Akhara Peethadishwar Swami Vishwadewanand was the centre of attraction it was completed on March the 25th, 2010. The religious head of Juna Akhara Maha Mandaleshwara Soham Baba, during Kumbh 2010 organised classes for the devotees and visitors to his camp and taught the people that nature is in fact the God. Soham Baba is an active and successful Neurologist and Micro surgeon, who in a very easy language stressed for the survival and protection of the environment as well as yoga penance Tantra and Mantra etc.

Uttarakhand's Chief Minister Dr. Ramesh Pokhariyal visited Kumbh 2010 to have a bath in the Ganges with his wife after midnight, without any security. Somehow police control cameras spotted him and officers rushed to assist him. His act of faith is praised by saints, administration, and many others.

Pilot Baba of Juna Akhara, who was an expert pilot in Indian Air Force attracted a large number of foreigners and devotees in his eye catching and his towering luxurious Pandal. A number of English speaking foreigners had translators and communicators with them while visiting the camp of a Sanyasis. Every pandal had arrangements to guide and communicate with the devotees guests and travellers.

The lecture delivered by a spiritual teacher of world fame Sri Sri Ravi Sankar attracted a large crowd and the sadhus in his camp. Beside the Pandals of these religious heads, the crowds wandered here and there with the Mela Pandals of a number of *Mantriks, Yagyaks* and *Tantriks*. Each of the Pandals and camps during Kumbh 2010 was beyond the description; no one was less then another in the display of monetary power and wealth.

It was on 20th of January when a combination of Sadhus wearing black cloth, white and saffron cloth were observed in Kumbh city for the first time. The famous Saint and Shani Dham Peethadhishwar - Maharaj Mahant Rajasthani was elected as Maha Mandeleshwar in a gathering organised in a camp of Panchayati Akhara at Kankhal. A number of Akharas rented helicopters for showering flowers on the Shahi Peshwai. It was not seen before in any Kumbh.

Media Centre

It was possible for the first time in the history of Kumbh that the huge media centre was provided for the journalists, photographers, cinematographers and other mediums of expression like computers, radio and social communication medium users. The latest and most modern computers, colour photo copiers, laser printers and fax facilities were available free of cost round the clock.

Temporary residential facility was provided for three hundred media persons and an open ground for meeting with more than 1500 media personnel.

Super fast broad band internet facilities were available for 100 media journalist. Apart from all these facilities a media centre was equipped with a modern audio video studio directly connected with the satellite, studio control room and an editorial section with a non-linear machine was also available. Road side cafes with reasonable rates and Hindi/English translators were available free of cost. For the first in the history of Kumbh Haridwar a high iron plated platform was made available fro camera persons at Hari ki Pairi and an extra platform was provided for other media person where bathing activities on the ghats were easily visible.

Historical Events at Haridwar Kumbh and Ardh Kumbh
In 1253, Fight between Naga Sanyasis and Vaishnawa Sadhus.
In 1310, Maha Nirvani Akhara Sadhus were on the next bank of the river Ganga at Neel Dhara near Nileshwar Mahadev Temple. About 22,000 Nagas of Maha Nirvani attacked on Rama Nandi Vaishnavas in Kankhal
In 1389, Amir Zafer Taimur looted Mayapuri at Haridwar
In 1393, Ardh Kumbh, Taimur Lung came to Haridwar during the Ardh Kumbh and looted the city. He killed thousands of persons and destroyed many temples.
In 1621, Ardha Kumbh, Emperor Jahangir observed killing and fight between Udasi and Vairagies
In 1628, Naga Sanyasis killed many Vairagees
In 1640, Fight between the Mundis (Vairagis) and Sanyasis (Naga)
In 1650, Naga Sanyasies killed Vairagis
In 1666, The Mughal Emperor Aurangazeb attacked the Kumbh, this attack was jointly faced by Naga Sanyasis and the Maratha soldiers
In 1760, Nearly 18000 Vairagi sadhus were killed in fight with the Naga sanyasis
In 1784, Sri Panchayati Akhara was established during the Kumbh
In 1796, Captain Thomas Hardwick visits Kumbh.5000 Sadhus were killed by Sikh Army of Patiala
In 1808, British traveller Feli Winset Raper wrote he never saw such number of pilgrims to bath at any other place
In 1819, Nearly 450 pilgrims were killed at Hari ki Pairi due to mismanagement

In 1840, One Christian observer visited Kumbh

In 1844, Demonstration of miraculous powers of Baba Shrawan Nath

In 1855, Establishment of Nirmal Panchayati Akhara, Bala Saheb Peshawa, Tatya Tope and others planned to uproot British Rule from India

In 1879, Internal dispute amongst the Akharas on the issue to bath first into the river resulted into killing of 500 Sadhus. The Akharas decided a bathing sequence to be followed.

In 1892, Ban imposed due to Cholera

In 1909, Mahatma Gandhi visited Kumbh and chalked out the non-cooperation Movement against the British

In 1915, Mahatma Gandhi visited during Kumbh at Haridwar he writes, '17 Lakhs visitors could not be hypocrites

In 1927, Uncontrolled crowd resulted in stampede causing number of deaths

In 1938, Fire broke out in a market across the river Ganga. The uncontrolled crowd killed many persons

In 1944, The British Government banned Kumbh due to war. The public decided to bear and share the arrangements and celebrated Kumbh

In 1962, Order of merit decided for Shahi Snan for Akharas

In 1986, The Chief Ministers from U.P., Bihar, Haryana visited for a sacred bath at Hari ki Pairi. An accident occurred due to blockage of the crowd on main passage.

In 1998, Conflict over the order of bathing sequence

In 2010, Few casualties were noticed during bathing at the event of third Shahi Snan but the situation was quickly controlled by the Mela Administration

The Akhara Parishad decided to participate in four Shahi Snans instead of three. It was on the 12th February that all the 13 Akharas together joined the first Shahi Snan setting aside their differences.

Rama Nand, (Managing Director, Pilgrims Publishing), says with a heavy heart, that he is extremely distressed to see the way our life-giving rivers are being polluted and poisoned, and are gradually drying up and becoming dirty drains.

Eons ago our sages had said, *"Jalam Jivanam"* (water is life). Even with all our education we have lost sight of this basic truth. We have to look after Nature if we expect to continue enjoying its fruits. We must not let the blind march for technological progress destroy our environment. Any imbalance that we create will only harm us. We need to think deeply about these issues which affect our lives. To make the Ganges and other rivers clean again, everyone will have to take a pledge to do their bit, and this should form part of our basic education. The scriptures say *"Ann Brahm"* (the grain is supreme). Man is what he eats, so if the grain is poisoned, it will affect all those who eat it in a negative way. That is why one talks of life-giving grains. Our villages still remain an ideal, where life revolves around agriculture and life is simple.

Rama Nand says when he asks the younger generation, "What is your aim in life", the answer usually is, "to make money, and still more money". He asks, why only money, to which the reply is, to be able to fulfil all our desires. At the same time this attitude is a source of dissatisfaction and unhappiness. They are driven to chasing large salary packages from multi-national companies and don't have the time to think of anything else. Money masters their lives, and in their race for making this money, they lose all relationships, and their health as well.

We need our youth to awaken and start leading meaningful lives, which are environment friendly and benefit mankind in general, so that everyone leads peaceful, satisfied, and happy lives. We must realize that the world is one, and all of us who leave in it, are inter-dependent.

Sandal is cooling
Cooler still is moonlight
But the coolest is Sadhu Satsang
So say the Scriptures

Mahant Ramanand Puri Ji Maharaj Niranjani Akhara

Junapeethadheeshwar Aacharya Avdheshanand Giri Ji

Shriman Shri Mahant Hariharanandji
Shri Panchayati Akhara Bada Udaseen

Shriman Mahant Shankardasji
Shri Panchayati Akhara Bada Udaseen

Shriman Mahant Maheshwardasji
Shri Panchayati Akhara Bada Udaseen

Shriman Mahant Raghumuniji
Shri Panchayati Akhara Bada Udaseen

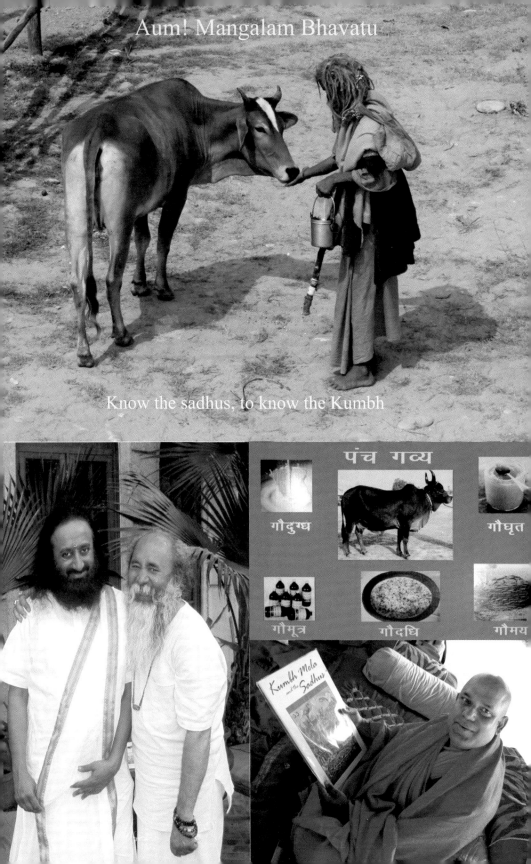

Aum! Mangalam Bhavatu

Know the sadhus, to know the Kumbh

पंच गव्य

गौदुग्ध

गौघृत

गौमूत्र

गौदधि

गौमय

Ram, Sita, Lakshman and Hanuman

Chaitanya Maha Prabhu

Pilgrim carrying the Ganga Jal

Sadhu

Vish kanya

Shrimati Sushma Swaraj, MP and Leader of Opposition (BJP), worshipping Maa Ganga

Ramesh Pokhriyal alongwith the All India BJP President Mr. Nitin Gadkari worshipping Maa Ganga

CM Dr. Ramesh Pokhariyal in a Press
Conference withTourism Minister
Shri Madan Kaushik after Inagurating the
Kumbh Mela Haridwar 2010

Chief Minister Dr. Ramesh Pokhariyal
commenting on the Posters set of
Kumbha Mela and Sadhu

Ganesh Baba, Crazy Baba, Rainbow Baba, Shiva Baba

Know the Time, Know the Body, Know the Nature and Space

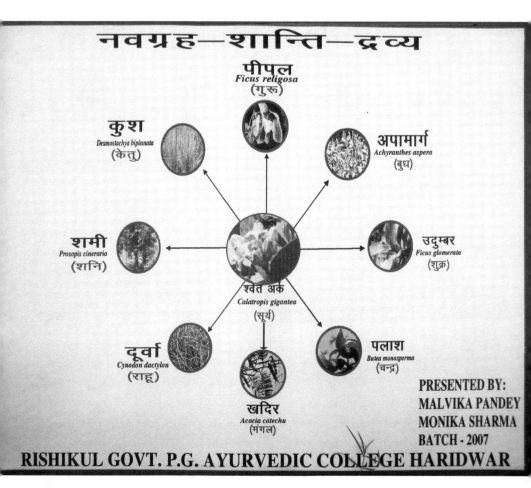

Lord of the Universe Jagannath Ji

Eunuchs (Neutrals) at Kumbh

Respect for Parents & to Serve them is the real Worship of God

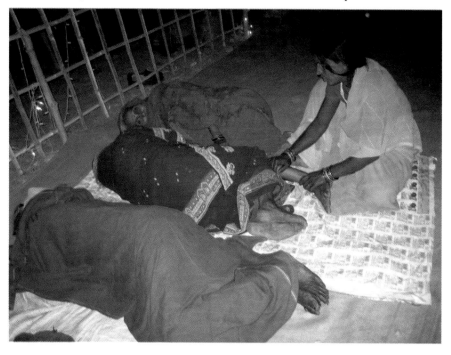

Maa Annapurna offering
the food to Lord Shiva

Sister serving the *prasaad* at
Soham Baba's camp

Offering of *Prasaad* to the pilgrims at Kumbh

129   *Kumbh Mela and the Sadhus*

Pilot Baba
पायलट बाबा

Q: "Is there One Message that you have for All of Humanity?"

Pilgrims

प्रश्न –
आपका मानबता के लिए क्या संदेश है?
– पिलग्रिम्स

Kumbh Mela
PILOT BABA CAMP, HARIDWAR 2010

कुम्भ मेला
पायलट बाबा शिबिर हरिद्वार २०१०

A: "Peace... only Peace. When you have Inner-Peace, Outer-Peace Happens..."

Pilot Baba

उत्तर –
'शान्ति और सिर्फ शान्ति! जब आपके पास आन्तरिक शान्ति होती है, तब बाह्य शान्ति स्वतः ही प्राप्त हो जाती है'।
– पायलट बाबा

Who Is Yogmata ?

YOGMATA KEIKO AIKAWA It is "Discovery of your own truth, divine identity". Living in the divine and merging within the whole. Nothing but feeling of "ONENESS " emerges in you. To know oneself through Samadhi is to meet one's true Self, it is the beginning of knowing Consciousness.

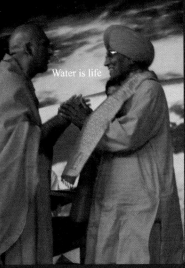

Water is life

Junapeethadheeshwar
Aacharya Avdheshanand Giri Ji
Swami Agnivesh Ji

समस्तः लोका सुखिः नो भवन्तु

महाकुम्भ 2010 में पतित पावनी गंगा में आचमन कर स्वयं को पूण्यार्थ करें।

ओउम् श्री साई राम

Service to Man kind
Service to God

मानव सेवा
माधव सेवा

श्री सत्य साई सेवा संगठन
उत्तराखंड एवं उत्तर प्रदेश

Jagannath
Lord of the universe

Maa Ganga Aarti & Bhajan at Parmarth Niketan, Rishikesh

Maa Ganga Aarti at Har Ki Pairi, Haridwar

Chapter 7
Kumbh, Sadhus and Salvation
Early Research by the Holy men in India
and the Theories of Salvation

Hindu monks, holy men and priests in India decoded the secrets of the universe and they created a science of religion. Death, suffering and old age were believed to result from personal actions and deeds or an act of God, which humans considered beyond their control, hence the need for salvation. The science of religion has been interpreted and adapted in many ways by different saints and schools of thought, each advocating various approaches to life and ways towards enlightenment, immortality and salvation. In ancient times they prayed *Tamso Ma Jyotirgamaya, Mrityor Ma Amritagamaya.* Let Nature move humanity from death to immortality.

Hindu religious science confirmed the fact of death or mortality of a creature's body along with the immortality of its invisible soul. Ancient religious text *Tandi Shruti* recorded the process of the soul's movement from one place to another after the physical body died.

The Vedas held five components (elements) of nature responsible for a living creator's physical body to emerge, *Chhita, Jala, Pawaka, Gagana* and *Samira*, (sky, air, fire, water and earth). These five elements of nature, simultaneously and sequentially producing the next when combined, form a physical body to be born through a womb.

The Birth and the Rebirth Theory

The theories of rebirth call for one's deeds to result in an accumulated *Paapa* or *Punya*. *Paapa*, or bad deeds, lead one to be reborn in a low status family whereas a *Punya*, or accumulated credit of good deeds and Worship as Pooja, Japa and Upwasaa, etc., leads one to avail a birth in a high dignity family which opens a way to salvation. The Hindu text portrays the reasons of birth in good and bad *Yonies* as being caused by one's collected lifetime deeds. The word *Yoni* meaning here a living-creature of three major classifications: God, man and animals. The birth theory further talks of a vicious circle of eighty-four lakh living creatures, called 'Yonies', from which birth occurs time and time again.

Contrary to rebirth theories based on the accumulated results of one's lifetime deeds, certain scholars claim it to be the result of three qualities of nature (Maya) as being Sattvic, Rajasic and/or Tamasic, to different degrees. The three distinct qualities of Sato, peaceful and airy clarity, Rajo, active or fiery excited, and Tamo, slow stability or heavy dullness, as combined and expressed in the nature of a person, cause a rebirth in

Kamdhenu the wish fulfilling cow

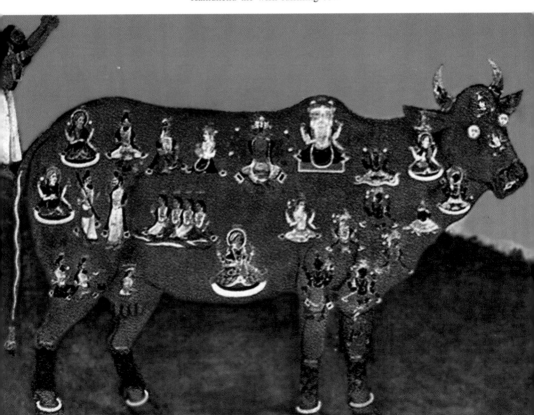

different Yonies after death. One who does not join the qualities of nature is never reborn.

Birth is narrated as *Janani Jathare Shayanama,* meaning sleeping inside the mother's womb.

The theory of *Panchagni Vidya* narrates of rebirth for the bodies that die during the period of *Dakshinayana*, meaning the Sun en route to the South Pole. A soul which leaves a body during this time period on the earth later receives a creature's body. The soul is first transformed through rainwater into different vegetables and herbs then, when eaten by a living creature, it metabolizes into semen and is reborn in the same type of Yoni as the creature by which it was eaten.

The soul further continues reincarnating to complete birth cycles experiencing the full range of eighty-four lakh living creatures. The crossing point of the birth cycle is a birth in the category of human beings, which one receives on completion of the primary birth cycle. The theory of the birth and rebirth was discovered and disclosed by the great scholars in 5000 BC.

Kamdhenu the wish fulfilling cow

Ways to Salvation
a) Salvation for the householder

A householder would normally avail salvation through Sanyas in old age. Yet there are four other ways for a householder to avail salvation without detaching from familial ties: (i) *Poojana*: worship of and to God, (ii) *Japa*: to memorize the name of God or deity, (iii) *Upwasaa*: to keep fast, and (iv) *Kashiwasa*: to reside in the sacred city of Kashi or to avail a death in Kashi.

Commenting on the theory of deeds and worship, the great teacher Shankaracharya was of the opinion that deeds and worship do not directly lead a soul to salvation. Deeds and worship only purify a physical body and heart to generate the feeling of the divine unseen power called God. It is the knowledge and purity of the body which unites the soul with the God and leads to salvation. A householder attains salvation or Moksha if he is mentally prepared to. He would opt for any of the opportunities available before him such as (i) to avail the great bath at Kumbh, (ii) to avail *Chhetra Sanyas* or reside in Varanasi, (iii) join one of the seven places of the pilgrimage or the *Tirtha,* (iv) have a holy dip in the river Ganga, (v) have a mere sight of the sacred river Ganga, (vi) avail the

Camping on Varanasi Ghats

sacred code after one's death as *Taraka Mantra* in Varanasi, (vii) continually recite the name of the Lord Rama, (viii) join a sacrifice (ix) join the *Poojan, Japa* and *Upwasa*, etc.

b) Salvation for the soul of an unreleased spirit

Bodies who die an unnatural death revolve in *Preta Yoni* for a considerably long time. The *Preta,* or unreleased spirit, depends on his family successors to enjoin certain rituals for its release. Some of the ways

are to hear the story of *Garuda Purana* and *Srimada Bhagwata Saptah*. Some follow to *Gaya Sharaddha* and *Pinda* for an unreleased spirit. One of the other ways to save an unreleased spirit is to drop the ashes of the dead body into the river Ganga.

c) Salvation for the soul of a holy man

A large number of India's population who accept an ascetic life detach themselves from family ties and appear in society as holy men and salvation seekers. To opt for an ascetic life is to join the fourth order of Hindu Ashrams, the fourth

Churning the Ocean

stage of life passages, as a Sanyas and to live as a novitiate for the rest of his life.

One who commits to Sanyas is called Sanyasi, synonymous to the word Sadhu. In the ancient books, it appears as Rishi, Muni, Vairagi, Tapaswi and Yogi, etc. Now the question is whether mere renunciation of worldly ties leads an ascetic's soul to salvation? What is the role of the deeds as great penance towards salvation? and when do they avail salvation?

There are two major branches of the ascetic's path in India. First is the *Avadhoota Pantha* of the deity Dattatreya and next is the *Vidwata Sanyas* of the great sage Sanaka Sanandana Sanatana and Sanata Kumara. Acceptance of Sanyas detaches one from worldly pleasures, possessions and ties.

Ascetics (Sadhus or Sanyasis) enjoin practices of penance or involve themselves in deeds of self-torture for the rest of their life. The deeds of penance by an ascetic may be (i) to rest in Samadhi, (ii) to hold a complete silence for twelve years, (iii) to accept meals after a time gap of several days or to subsist on only milk, (iv) to expose the body to air, water or fire or bury any of the organs underground, (v) lifting weight with the genital organs, (vi) to raise one's hands or stand all night and day, sleep on thorny beds, etc.

Others believe that a result oriented deed does not result in detachment so causes rebirth.The great teacher Shankaracharya was of the opinion that deeds of penance as worship bring purity to the physical body which further unites one's soul to the God. Hence a living creature avails salvation through the knowledge that he is at one with the divine creation power *Brahma*. He said, 'No knowledge, no salvation.' A body who gains the supreme knowledge avails *Jiwan Mukti* or salvation within one's life.

Apart from the Sanyasis and the Aghoris, there are the Vaishnava Sadhus (followers of Lord Vishnu) who claim salvation only for householders or *Sansari* people. According to them, salvation is not the ultimate object of an ascetic. They say an ascetic, a Sadhu or a Vairagi joins so many cycles

Kumbh in Ujjain 2004 (Olaf Rocksien)

of rebirths to earn the high post of *Siya Rama*, i.e., they put their life in great penance aiming at a number of birth cycles to serve God. They say the *Sant* reappear as saints, every time they change their mortal body. In support of their claim, they quote the lines of the sacred book *Ramayana*, '*Aartha na, Dharma na, Kalama ruche, gati na chahaun Nirvana, Janama Janama SiyaRama Pad yaha Vardaan...*' Meaning they do not aim at the worldly desires for money, religion, sex or salvation except to serve God for many lives and births. Still the great Indian author and Vaishnava saint, Goswami Tulsi Das, mentions that the saints practiced penance for a long time but the name of the God did not come from their mouth even at the last moment.

Chanting to practice the name of the God for salvation

The religious texts advocate to practice chanting the name of God for the soul, at the time of rebirth, remembers the time of prior death. If by practice and habit, the soul remembers the name of God in one's last hours, it is not diverted to matters of illusion (Maya) during the crucial time, hence avails salvation. The body remembers the divine God, his soul joins the divine power and is never reborn.

Salvation by mere sight of the sacred river Ganga

The holy texts tell us that the mere sight of the main river Ganga bestows salvation to a devotee. A droplet of the holy river Ganga water poured into the mouth of a dying person leads him to salvation. Even if the ashes from one's cremated corpse are dropped into the river Ganga, it leads the dead soul to salvation. A sacred bath, dipping in the river Ganga, bestows salvation to a bather and his family, even unto seven generations past.

Salvation through a death in seven sacred cities

The religious texts propose that a householder may move toward salvation via a natural death in one of the seven sacred places of pilgrimage called the Tirtha. Of the seven Tirtha cities, six cities, Ayodya, Mathura, Haridwar, Kanchi, Awantika (Ujjain), Puri and Dwarika cause one to avail a future birth in Kashi for only Kashi is capable of providing full salvation to souls who die within its limits.

Salvation only in the holy city Kashi (Benares or Varanasi)

The holy city called *Awimukta Chhetra* bestows salvation to a living creature. Even in the final day of destruction, *Pralaya*, the Lord of the universe Shiva does not leave Kashi. The holy city during the period of *Pralaya* existed separate to this universe. On the authority of Lord Vishnu, in his first incarnation as *Varaha Awatara*, the earth was released from under the water and combined to the holy city of Kashi. The word *Awi* in *Linga Purana* is described as a sin; hence the place devoid of sins and with a capacity to remove sin is *Awimukta Chhetra,* i.e., a region to get rid of one's sins. One prepared to reside within the territory of the holy city Varanasi with a willingness to avail a natural death is said to have accepted *Chhetra Sanyas*. It is a renunciation of one's dwelling region other than the city Kashi..

The Vedas term it a sight which is visible throughout the holy city as, here, the human eyes are able to see the truth regarding the existence of the false and perishable universe. Since the holy city Kashi is everlasting, it is the only place to avail salvation by death. Even the body of a human being who died elsewhere, if brought to the city of Kashi for funeral rites, avails salvation by combination of the holy city Kashi with the holy river Ganga and the sacred code *Taraka Mantra*.

The sacred code of *Taraka Mantra* is *Rama Naam*—the name of God, which Lord Shiva, patron deity of Varanasi, whispers in the ears of the dead body , as soon as it is brought to the cremation ghat, *Manikarnika*.

One who dies in Kashi receives four varieties of salvation at a time: (i) direct achievement of the place of the God, i.e. *Salokya Mukti*, in *Shivaloka* (ii) direct attainment of a state unlike God, i.e., *Sarupya Mukti*, (iii) direct achievement to reside near God, i.e., *Sanidhya Mukti*, (iv) to untie from Maya or the affections, i.e., *Kaivalya Mukti*.

Life salvation and Supreme salvation

The religious leader Shankaracharya further propagated *Parama Mukti,* a supreme salvation, i.e., a stage after the life salvation. According to him, a being avails this supreme salvation as a final salvation, when the soul leaves the body after the death of the physical body. A holy-man in a sense avails both the *Jivan Mukti*, salvation in now and the *Parama Mukti*, supreme soul salvation upon death, thus he finishes the cycle of birth and death in this universe.

Har-Har Mahadev

* the boundries of this map of India are not authentic.

Kumbh Mela and the Sadhus

MORE TITLES ON HINDUISM / CULTURE
AND THE KUMBH

- The Yogini Temples of India: In the Pursuit of a Mystery............*Stella Dupuis*
- Sacred Symbols of Hinduism..*J R Santiago*
- Myths and Legends of India..*J M Macfie*
- Sadhus of India ....*B D Tripathi*
- Hindu Manners, Customs and Ceremonies ....*by Abbe J A Dubois*
- Modern Hinduism...*W J Wilkins*
- Philosophy of Hindu Sadhana................................*Nalini Kanta Brahma*
- The Foundation of Hinduism..*Jadunath Sinha*
- Popular Hinduism..*By L S S O'Malley*
- Hindu Holidays and Ceremonies ....*B. A. Gupte*
- Hindu Gods and Goddesses................................... *Harendr Upadhyay*
- The Kumbh Mela ....*Mark Tully*
- Kumbh Mela ....*Ashin Ghosh*
- Indian Sadhus ....*G. S. Ghurye*
- Sadhu ....*Rakesh Bedi*
- Discovery of India ....*Pt. Jawahar Lal Nehru*
- Ascetics of Kashi ....*Sinha and Saraswati*

For more information visit our websites
pilgrimsbooks.com and pilgrimsonlineshop.com
or contact us for catalogs at the addresses given below.

PILGRIMS BOOK HOUSE
B. 27/98 A-8 Nawab Ganj Road
Durga Kund Varanasi 221010
Tel: 91-542-2314060
Fax: 91-542-2312456
E-mail: pilgrimsbooks@sify.com

PILGRIMS BOOK HOUSE
(New Delhi)
2391, Tilak Street, Chuna Mandi,
Paharganj,
New Delhi 110055
Tel: 91-11-23584015
Fax: 91-11-23584019
E-mail: pilgrimsinde@gmail.com

PILGRIMS BOOK HOUSE
(Kathmandu)
P O Box 3872, Thamel,
Kathmandu, Nepal
Tel: 977-1-4700942
Off: 977-1-4700919
Fax: 977-1-4700943
E-mail: pilgrims@wlink.com.np